SKELETONS IN THE MEDICAL CLOSET

A Personal Story and Professional Report

Medical Errors, Hospital Mistakes

By

Meyer Sonis, M.D.

A PAFIP Publication

Copyright © 2001 by Meyer Sonis M.D.
All rights reserved.
No part of this book may be reproduced, stored in a retrieval system, or transmitted by any means, electronic, mechanical, photocopying, recording, or otherwise, without written permission from the author.

ISBN 0-75963-223-5

This book is printed on acid free paper.

1stBooks – rev. 07/10/01

Dedicated to My Wife

and

Physician Advocates for
Informed Patients

TABLE OF CONTENT

Table Of Content v

Foreword ix

An opinion about this book by Dr. C. Everett Koop and his wife Elizabeth Koop following their review of the book.

Introduction xiii

A statement by the author regarding the background for his writing of this book and his objective in so doing, namely to provide a lay targeted audience with information and data about their medical care so that they can become informed patients.

Chapter One A Personal Story 1

The recounting by this physician author of his own personal experiences with the various skeletons in the medical closet during his wife's hospitalization and her unanticipated death. These experiences serve as an example for the topics reported on in subsequent chapters.

Chapter Two Medical Injuries, Medical Errors 31

Based on his nine year investigation of the published scientific and clinical literature on medical care and its quality, the author renders his professional report on the results of this investigation. The skeletons in the medical closet which are reported include the topics of adverse events and medical injuries, adverse drug reactions and adverse drugs events, medical errors and negligence, failures in and of hospitals, medical malpractice.

<u>Chapter Three</u> Lessons To Be Learned.. 56

Based on his professional experience as a medical educator and administrator, as well as on his review of pertinent literature, the author will utilize this chapter to share his opinion on the lessons to be learned from the occurrence of "bad things" which can happen to patients during the provision of medical and hospital care. These are the lessons about system and human failure in medical errors and the lessons to be learnt by physicians, medical educators, hospitals, licensing and accreditation authorities, as well as the patient himself or herself.

<u>Chapter Four</u> The Physician Industry.. 75

In light of the significant role which the physician plays in the rendering of sound or shoddy medical care, it behooves the informed patient to learn about the physician industry as one component of the medical-industrial complex. Information and data will be presented about physician facts and characteristics of medical practice, undergraduate medical education, medical schools, medical students, medical educators, post graduate medical education, physician generalists and specialists, income and expenses and fees of physicians.

<u>Table 1</u>   Geographic Distribution Of All Physicians In The United States 82

<u>Chapter Five</u> The Hospital Industry 111

In light of the significant role which the hospital plays in the rendering of safe or unsafe hospital care, it also behooves the informed patient to learn about the hospital industry as another component of the medical-industrial complex. Information and data will be presented about the emergence of the modern hospital in the United States, the types and categories of hospitals, the operation and structure of a hospital from owners to management/medical staff/nurses/professional services/pharmacy/ "watchdog" medical activities/medical services.

<u>Chart</u>: Model Of Hospital Organization 133

<u>Chapter Six</u> Who Watches The Doctor And Hospital 154

In keeping with the need for the informed patient to be assured of safety, competence and quality in the medical and hospital care which they secure, it is important for this informed patient to know about the various watchdogs over medical care and the effectiveness of this monitoring. Information and data will be presented about self-policing by physicians, the various activities of a hospital which are aimed at looking over the shoulder of caregivers, the monitoring of medical care by the State boards of Medical Licensure/accreditation authorities/ governmental bodies/legal profession/the consumers.

<u>Epilogue</u> 178

A brief note of gratitude from the author to those who created the information and data on which I reported and to those who encouraged the writing of this book.

<u>Appendix A</u> Bibliographic References 179

A listing of those sources from which information and data was secured for each chapter.

<u>Appendix B</u> Informed Patient Resources 196

A listing of various sources available to the informed patient from which the informed patient can secure information to learn about their health, medical conditions, and medical care.

<u>Letter To My Readers</u> 202

A plan by the author for the future development of a Physician Advocate For Informed Patient Program (PAFIP), which will supplement the objective of this book, namely, to inform patients about their health, health behavior, medical problems, and medical care.

Foreword

Skeletons in the Medical Closet

We were for many years close friends of the author of this book, Mike Sonis, and his wife Anne, whose tragic encounter with the medical industry prompted this report. We were close to Mike through the trying days of Anne's terminal illness. As we watched the unfolding story depicted here, our dismay turned to outrage because here was an intelligent couple that did everything they could before hospitalization to ensure its safety, and Mike and his two sons, all physicians, were all aware of what can happen in medical situations.

Mike wrote this book in an era when doctors did not talk much about medical error. This is still the case, but there's been a steady drumbeat on the part of some of us in medicine about the problem of medical error and its prevention. It has certainly been a part of my lectures on health care reform for the last five or six years.

The intent of the author was to make available to informed patients, or those about to be patients, just how easily one can fall through the cracks during a hospitalization in spite of every preparation to prevent that. He then did a considerable service for all of us by including an extraordinarily complete report of his personal story, the meaning of terms such as medical error, hospital mistakes, medical negligence, and medical malpractice, the physician industry, the hospital industry, and then he asks the most pertinent question: "Who watches the doctor and the hospital?" An epilogue, two helpful appendices and a letter to the reader complete the treatise.

In late 1999, the National Academy of Sciences published a report on medical error entitled "To Err Is Human" and aroused the media to call to the public's attention the fact of medical error. Public awareness of the consequences of medical error should make this a welcome book. It not only examines in the light of the Sonis tragedy the anatomy of medical error but also reveals the negligence that made it possible, the callous indifference of the medial culprits in their legal testimony, the dereliction of duty on the part of the office of the Inspector General of the Department of Health and Human Services, whose interest should have been significant because Medicare paid for shoddy care, and finally the lackadaisical attitude of the lawyers who had the opportunity to at least set the record straight even though they could not bring back the life of the patient.

When I was a resident surgeon, one of the best teaching times for me was the weekly morbidity and mortality conference. The hospital where I trained had two surgical services and therefore we were in a friendly, but critical situation when we reported our mistakes to one another. In other words, we were not in a position where we could whitewash them. We discussed every patient death, every critically ill patient, and every mistake that we knew about. It was the individual surgeon's obligation to diagnose the cause of the problem under discussion in one of the following ways: patient's disease, act of God, error in management, error in judgment, error in technique or institutional error. In this way, nothing was hidden; everything was in the open. We learned from our mistakes and made every effort to prevent them from ever happening again.

Then one day, two of the hospital lawyers arrived unexpectedly at our meeting and told us that in the future, we should not keep minutes because those minutes could be subpoenaed by a lawyer for a plaintiff suing the hospital and/or one of its doctors and we had to prevent all of the malpractice suits that we could. Shortly thereafter, they further instructed us not to have the meetings at specific prearranged times, but to have them on an ad hoc basis. Obviously, the system fell apart, and the one chance we had to institutionalize the study of error disappeared with it.

The present malpractice system in America does not work. It does not work for the patient; it does not work for the physician. The underlying problem is that error does occur in medicine. But we don't deal with error in medicine as we should. The reasons lie in the combination of the dictum that "to err is human" and the extremely complicated nature of medical interventions, combined with the fear of a malpractice suit.

Fortunately, most errors can be corrected, but when they do lead to tragic outcome, the effect is devastating, notably on the patient and patient's family, but also on the doctor and other health care workers.

The problem of error is intensified by the general culture of medicine, which has not found effective ways to deal with errors, to learn from errors, to prevent errors. Physicians are trained and operate in a culture that demands perfection, but where mistakes are not only inevitable, but also inadmissible.

Obviously, the current threat of malpractice litigation almost eliminates the opportunity to disclose error, to learn from mistakes, and to receive support from colleagues and even patients when inevitable errors do occur. By sweeping the issue under the rug, medicine is not taking advantage of ways to make institutional structural changes in training and practice that could go a long way to reduce the number of medical errors.

Having said all that, we have to conclude the author's description that Anne Sonis did not die of the ordinary medical error that everyone tries to prevent. Anne Sonis died because of the lack of close attention by her surgeon to her individual response to the surgery. The resident did not keep him fully informed, sharing with him the concern she should have had about her patient's downhill course. But the resident also seemed callous, unaware of imminent danger, and unwilling to rally what support was available.

Mike Sonis and his two sons, Bill and Jeff, were all knowledgeable, experienced and understanding physicians, particularly concerned about Anne well before her hospital admission, and especially during her downhill course. Anne herself was a proponent of quality assurance and the necessity of an informed patient. No patient could have gone into her surgical experience better prepared and with better family support. At a time when every force should have been marshaled to bring the best of medical science to bear on her problem, the system failed Anne and her family at every turn.

The chapter on legal affairs is not only chilling but roused in us a sense of outrage. No one in the legal profession seemed to care about the outcome, and the responsible surgeon shunned all responsibility for his resident's behavior. In medicine, as at sea, the captain of the ship is responsible for the behavior of the crew.

This is a riveting book to read, although it depicts a human tragedy. In these days of slackened responsibility, meager compassion, and dulled sensitivity, let the public be aware of the pitfalls that can occur in a complicated hospital experience. Fortunately, situations such as described here are rare, but the supportive material that Mike Sonis has prepared for his reader is invaluable for anyone who faces hospitalization for self or a loved one.

Medical error can take place in spite of the effort of a medical team to do its best. This is a different story; it is medical error due to negligence and incompetence, defended by medical and legal indifference. There is, unfortunately, no recourse. It is a tribute to their mental and emotional stability that the family has been able to carry on with their lives. In addition the author has given the reader cause for diligence along with some supportive guidelines when presented with serious elective surgery. Caveat emptor.

C. Everett and Elizabeth Koop

INTRODUCTION

In conceiving and preparing this book it has been my intent to address several targeted audiences with information about the Skeletons in the Medical Closet, such as medical errors, medical negligence, hospital mistakes, adverse events.

The information to be shared will be focused on these "bad things" which can happen to a patient during their process of receiving medical and hospital care, and on the doctors and hospitals who and which are the potential perpetrators and setting for these "bad things," and on the persons or agents or agencies who and which serve as "watchdogs" over doctors and hospitals.

In conveying this information I will do so through two conduits, namely, a personal story and a professional report.

The personal story which I will recount will be about my wife's unanticipated death due to several "bad things" which occurred to her during her hospitalization. In telling this story I do not do so because of the unusual nature of the bad things which happened to her or because of the specialness of the persons in the story. Rather, I do so because this story can serve as an illustration of the information to be shared in the professional report and does reflect the many untold stories of persons and families who also hurt as a consequence of the sad outcome of medical and hospital care.

The professional report to be given will be based on documented information about these Skeletons In The Medical Closet, the reasons for such skeletons, the doctors and hospitals and their "watchdogs" and the lessons to be learned. This report will be rendered not because of the "newness" of the revelations but rather because of the need to bring the skeletons out of the medical closet where they have been hidden by a conspiracy of silence.

The first of the two intended target audiences which I hope to address through this book will be the several different categories of lay persons who potentially can become a casualty of their medical and hospital care.

I am, for one, referring to the lay persons who already are informed patients. These are the persons who: seek information about their health, medical and hospital care, and beyond that of the sound bytes of media reports about wrong amputations, wrong surgery, wrong medication; are knowledgeable about resources and sources for pertinent information; avail themselves of help from patient advocate agencies. These are the persons who are the buyers and readers of books, the internet browsers who are privy to pertinent information in government publications, the New Yorker magazine, the Sunday New York Times. These are the persons who feel comfortable asking questions of their doctors and hospitals.

I am, for another, referring to the lay persons who are interested in becoming an informed patient and for this reason are willing and capable of taking the steps needed to acquire and learn about pertinent information. These are the persons who can avail themselves of information beyond the "sound bytes" and three minute in depth television news. These are the persons who can be helped to see merit in becoming a knowledgeable partner in their own medical care.

But I am especially referring to those lay persons who are vulnerable to becoming a casualty of their medical care because of their economic, social, health literacy status. These are the persons who many times fall between the cracks of the medical care system and who can be identified in substantial numbers within the network of community human services. These are the lay persons who, if they are to become informed patients, are very dependent on the professional and technical staff of the human service agencies for help.

The second category of audience to be addressed through this book is that of the professional and technical cadre of human service practitioners. I am referring to the physicians, nurses, social workers, psychologists, counselors and other staff who now are responsible for delivery of medical, social, welfare, correctional, educational services. These are the persons who can be advocates for an informed patient; these are the persons who can disseminate pertinent information required by lay persons in becoming informed patients; these are the persons who can translate the medical jargon of books, journals, magazines into the user friendly language of the lay person. These are the persons who may be more amenable to serving as advocates for informed patients because they are in the process of learning to become physicians, social workers, counselors, nurses, psychologists and prior to becoming set in their behavior as professionals. It is this cadre of professional and technical human service practitioners who must be reached before they become "burned out."

Therefore, if the targeted audience are to be helped to become more informed professional care takers or more informed patients, then new paths must be found by which the medical information highway can reach them. Thus it behooves those who generate medical information (such as the clinicians, research scientists), and those who disseminate medical information (such as medical writers, medical educators, newspaper reporters), and those who distribute medical information (such as publishers, websites, newspapers, magazines, media networks) to find these new paths for the medical information highway to flow.

It is towards this end that I have written this book. It is towards this end that I will seek publication of this book. And finally it is towards this end that upon publication of this book, I will initiate my Physician Advocates For Informed Patients (PAFIP) program, which I describe in a letter to my reader.

*Skeletons in the Medical Closet*
A Personal Story and a Professional Report

CHAPTER ONE

A PERSONAL STORY

It is now ten years since my wife died a wrongful death while hospitalized and since I had personally entered the world of medical errors, hospital mistakes, and medical injuries which were occurring to patients including those who were physicians and /or their families.

At the time of my wife's death Anne was 68 years of age. I was 70 years of age and had been a physician for 46 years. We had been married for 45 years, following a three year courtship while I completed medical school and Anne completed college. Thus, Anne and I had a life separate from each other for only one third of our lives. Our three children were on their own, with two as physicians and one as a professional actress. Following upon my wife's death, and with the encouragement of an esteemed friend and colleague I wrote and published for private distribution a book entitled A Doctor Who Hurts. For purposes of this Chapter I will be abstracting from and adding to A Doctor Who Hurts.

Before Hospitalization

As a consequence of my wife's bout with rheumatic fever (an infection of the heart) as a child and adolescent she manifested a mitral valve (one of four heart valves) problem which necessitated routine antibiotics to prevent or minimize intercurrent infections. Ultimately, her cardiac condition stabilized allowing her to return to full activities, including completion of college, swimming, pregnancy and delivery of three children without complications, maintaining fulltime employment. She also became a member of the modern dance team at college and continued practice of such for a number of years.

Throughout Anne's adulthood, she became a very informed and compliant patient. She periodically had contact with her internist, cardiologist, gynecologist, and dentist. She was administered antibiotics when she had an infection. She would secure information from the medical school library regarding her cardiac status and intercurrent illnesses, whether these were bronchitis, diarrhea of unknown etiology, irritable bowel, or benign cyst of the breast. She stopped smoking seventeen years before her death.

In 1982, seven years prior to her hospitalization and following our last year of living abroad, she began to experience dyspnea (shortness of breath) on moderate exertion. Under the care of her internist and cardiologist, she undertook a series of studies, including a cardiac catheterization (insertion of tube into heart for infusion of dye) which ultimately led to the diagnosis of cardiac valve damage of moderate proportions due to her past rheumatic heart disease. Her coronary artery vessels (blood to heart muscle) were normal. She was placed on a standard conservative medical regime of medication, periodic echocardiograms (sonic study of heart valves) to assess cardiac valve size, cardiological consultation, and limited activities. Her dyspnea was controlled for a period of time and she did not experience dyspnea during sleep. Over the next three years, she ultimately began to manifest periodic reoccurrences of atrial fibrillation (cardiac arrhythmia, which often occurs with a rheumatic heart) requiring short periods of hospitalization and medical intervention in order to convert her arrhythmia to a normal sinus rhythm. Though her cardiologist did raise the possibility of surgery for mitral valve replacement at some future time, he did not recommend such but followed a conservative approach. This included continued medication, limited activities, watchful waiting by serial echocardiograms in order to assess mitral valve functions. Because of the increased frequency of her atrial fibrillation and with no change for the better in her pattern of dyspnea, my wife and I did our homework. We requested and secured a second opinion, from an expert in another city, regarding her current status. Following up on this second opinion consultation, we were advised that surgery should now be considered because of the progression in her cardiac valve problem. We transferred her medical care to another hospital in Pittsburgh.

As typical of Anne's realistic view of life my wife suggested that, since my risk for sudden death (because of coronary artery disease) was greater than her risk for sudden death, I should undertake the recommended bypass surgery first so that I could then be available to support her through her cardiac surgery. Following my recovery from a coronary artery bypass graft (surgical repair of heart arteries) and our return to Pittsburgh, my wife and I, and our children, began our homework in preparation for my wife's ultimate cardiac surgery. We reviewed the most recent literature on mitral valve replacement, we researched the various hospitals in our city regarding their "published" data on the volume of cardiac surgery they performed, their mortality rate for this surgery and the reputation of their surgical staff. We also secured opinions of other colleagues. Consequently, Anne felt most comfortable with the hospital in which her current cardiologist and internist practiced, and her family agreed with her decision.

We made arrangements for cardiac catheterization in preparation for cardiac surgery. The cardiac catheterization was successfully completed with no untoward reaction as she had experienced during her first catheterization. The diagnosis confirmed the studies done by the second opinion consultant, namely, my wife showed evidence of cardiac valve damage of moderate proportions which now required surgery. A member of the cardio-thoracic surgery department of the hospital provided consultation to my wife and her family following the catheterization. He recommended mitral valve replacement and reviewed the procedure, the risks and the benefits. He indicated that any member of the cardio-thoracic surgery team was capable of such cardiac surgery. Based on our "homework" we indicated our interest in securing the services of a specific surgeon who enjoyed an excellent reputation because of his experience. Interestingly, his skill and rapidity in surgery had earned him the title of "Sewing Machine."

Hospitalization

Once we had decided on and made arrangements with the cardiac surgeon, I wrote to him indicating our desire to personally meet with him and review Anne's situation with him. In preparation for this meeting I submitted an outline of Anne's past medical history to the cardiac surgeon. Unfortunately, this meeting was difficult to arrange due to the out of town and operating schedule of the cardiac surgeon. His office suggested that in light of the difficulty we were having in arranging for a meeting we meet the surgeon at the hospital after she was admitted. Because my wife and I felt rather strongly that we should meet the cardiac surgeon personally, and before the surgery if possible, we finally agreed to meet with him at his office just prior to her formal admission to the hospital. At this consultation he reviewed the situation with us and informed us that in his opinion the benefits of this surgery would far outweigh the risks. In keeping with this view of his, he indicated his intent to utilize a prosthetic (synthetic) heart valve rather than a porcine (pig) valve because this would probably minimize the need for a replacement during her anticipated life span of fifteen more years. Further, he allayed our anxiety about having such major surgery performed prior to the limited coverage schedule during the weekend.

On the day prior to her scheduled surgery, my wife was in good spirits and was realistically prepared for the surgery. Our three children were with us, as was my wife's brother, also a physician. Other family members visited. During that day, my

Skeletons in the Medical Closet
A Personal Story and a Professional Report

wife indicated that we had made a correct decision to have this done since she did not want to become a cardiac "cripple," a "vegetable," or a burden to all of us. My own successful experience with the bypass machine and intubation (tube into lung for maintaining breathing) and the medical publications which Anne had read seemed to act as guidelines for what was to be expected. I remained alone with my wife during the latter part of the evening while we discussed our plans for future travel and my ultimate retirement. In fact, in anticipation of positive results from this surgery, we had arranged to rent an apartment for two months in Florida during the coming winter. Anne and I had never taken a winter vacation. Before I left, she requested I get her a milk shake as a treat, which she "slurped" down with relish. On the day of the surgery, our children and I came to see Anne prior to her departure for the operating room so that we could speak with each other and wish her well. I did not know then that this would be the last opportunity for my wife to speak directly to me and for me to hear my wife's unique voice.

My family and I awaited the results of her surgery in the designated waiting room, as did the families of other patients. To our surprise, since we had anticipated a long wait, the cardiac surgeon came to us within two to three hours after her admission to surgery and with pleasure indicated that all had gone well and without complication. He showed us the cardiac valve which he had replaced. He indicated the correctness of our decision to undertake surgery in light of the state of valve calcification. He informed us that my wife would be in the surgical intensive care unit for up to two days, as was their routine, but that we would be able to see her for a bit in the morning and in the evening.

We were able to visit my wife after her return from the recovery room. At that time, she was still sedated from the anesthesia and fully equipped with all of the paraphernalia of an intensive care unit. We abided by the rules of visiting but remained in the area for the remainder of day one. Though she was becoming more responsive and awake and seemed to be progressing as expected, concern was expressed by the nursing and house staff (residents) about the continued "oozing" of blood from her mediastinal chest tube (tube to drain blood following surgery). This necessitated continued blood transfusions. At one point during day one (the day of operation), her cardiac surgeon informed us that if the oozing did not diminish it might be necessary to consider a return to surgery in order to locate the source of bleeding and correct it. Fortunately by day two, the oozing diminished. [However, it should be noted that on my review of my wife's hospital record, which I secured after her death, I learned of the seriousness of this so-called "oozing." The record documented that: immediately after the closure of the incision and while in the operating room, considerable oozing came from the wound which required application of topical coagulants; on day one, there was a serious loss of fluid volume over a twenty-four hour period of time (3500 cubic centimeters or half of her normal body fluid volume) requiring extensive transfusions and infusions. The record showed that there was a laboratory report of abnormal prothrombin (bleeding) time early on day one. However, this report was not followed up with other such laboratory studies in order to guide decisions about transfusions. The record also indicated the concern of her surgeon about possible cardiac tamponade (blood filling up the sac containing the heart) and the possible return to surgery.]

By day two, as stated, the oozing of blood had begun to diminish. My wife was more alert and responsive to us, though still intubated so that she could not speak. We were encouraged to believe that perhaps matters would now progressively advance to extubation (removal of breathing tubes) and discharge from the surgical intensive care unit.

At the time of our early evening visit on day three, however, we were very frightened and concerned by the situation which we found. My wife looked distressed and terror stricken. She seemed and looked as if in respiratory distress. My two physician sons described her stare as "air hunger" and they noted on the monitor that she had an elevated temperature, increased respiratory rate, and atrial fibrillation which had not been there previously. A nurse informed us that my wife had taken this turn for the worse in the afternoon. My sons were concerned about pneumonia (lung infection) and requested to speak with the resident on call. While my daughter and I remained with my wife, my sons spoke with the resident regarding their concern about pneumonia. They asked if blood and sputum cultures (to identify bacteria), a chest x-ray and a sputum gram stain (to identify bacteria) had been performed. The resident informed them that she had taken a blood culture, as called for on their protocol if a patient's temperature exceeded a certain mark. She did not believe pneumonia was present and saw no cause for alarm since atelectasis (collapse of lung air sacs) occurred quite frequently post-cardiac surgery. She did not see any need for further studies. My sons registered their concerns about my wife's condition with her primary nurse and informed the nurse of the resident's reluctance to follow up on their concerns regarding the possible diagnosis of pneumonia.

Our concern caused us to remain in the waiting area beyond the time allotted for visitors. Because of our continued anxiety, upon our return home that evening on day three, my son called my wife's cardiologist with whom we had an excellent relationship. Unfortunately he was not on call so my son talked with his partner on call and shared his concern about possible pneumonia and informed him about the discussion which had been held with the cardiac surgical resident. This on-call cardiologist indicated that, because the resident was not on his service, he would not interfere but informed my son that if we chose to we could go over the resident's head to her superior. In the hope that I could prevail, because of my seniority and status as the husband of the patient, I made a call to the resident at 11:00 P.M. on day three and shared my concerns regarding the condition of my wife. In response, she informed me that we were all over-concerned and that my wife's condition was one

Meyer Sonis M.D.

that was frequently seen post-operatively and that it would be relieved upon productive suctioning of the lung, which they were then doing. She indicated that the best thing we could do for my wife was to get a good night's sleep. My sons and I realized that we could possibly be over-anxious and that if we went over the resident's head to her superior, my wife could pay a price in her care by the potential hostility of the resident. We decided to wait, but we did inform the primary nurse on the intensive care unit that we wanted to be kept informed if matters deteriorated during the night. [On review of my wife's hospital record following her death, we were able to confirm the validity of the concerns we had expressed to the resident on call about the possibility of pneumonia. In this record we found: nurses' notes regarding sputum changes associated with a lung infection from day one to day two to day three; laboratory studies showing an elevated white blood cell count (associated with an infection) on days two and three which precipitously dropped on day four to a seriously low count; nurses' notes indicating a copious amount of bloody fluid looking like "coffee-like grounds" (associated with bleeding) flowing from the nasogastric tube (tube through nose to stomach) at 2:00 P.M. on day three; the computer log which documented the sudden increase in temperature, respiratory rate, poor respiratory gas exchange, and a shift from a sinus cardiac rhythm to atrial fibrillation at about 2:00 P.M. to 3:00 P.M. on day three; nurses' notes indicating labored breathing, restlessness and agitation at 2:00 P.M. on day three.]

On day four at 6:00 A.M., I called the surgical intensive care unit and was shocked to learn that my wife's condition had deteriorated so that she was in a critical state and awaiting an emergency bedside bronchoscopic examination. On our arrival at 7:30 A.M. on day four at the bedside of my wife, who had now been moved to an isolated cubicle of the intensive care unit, we found my wife's surgeon, my wife's cardiologist, and the pulmonologist (lung specialist) in serious conversation while awaiting the infectious disease consultant. My wife was heavily sedated and was not responsive. The bronchoscopic (tube into lung to see directly) examination revealed no obstructions (associated with atelectasis) but blood secretions from the lobe of the right lung. The surgeon informed us that my wife was in a serious state of crisis due to her septic shock (shock from overwhelming infection) and hypoxia (insufficient blood oxygen) which had not been recognized by the resident on call and had been aggravated by fluid loss through continued diuretic medication during the early morning hours of day four. For this reason, the surgeon and the cardiologist attempted to correct the situation by massive fluid infusions. The surgeon informed us that he had unfortunately not been notified of my wife's deterioration by the resident on call until that morning; we were informed by the cardiologist that he had discovered the crisis on his early morning rounds (6:00 A.M. on day four) and that it had been he who had instructed the resident on call to inform her superior and to secure consultation from the pulmonary and infectious disease specialists. Following consultation from the infectious disease specialist, he ordered a chest x-ray, blood cultures and a sputum gram stain. It was decided that the presumptive diagnosis was necrotizing pseudomonas (type of bacteria) pneumonia, septic shock (shock from overwhelming infection) and hypoxia and that a more appropriate antibiotic and dosage be initiated beyond the antibiotic given at 1:00 A.M. on day four by the resident on call. [Only upon review of the medical record following my wife's death did the sequence of events leading to this crisis become clear. At midnight on day four, a chest x-ray was ordered but there was no documentation that it was performed or read. In fact, this x-ray could not be found on my later inquiry. At 1:00 A.M. on day four, the resident on call initiated an antibiotic because of my wife's elevated temperature and poor respiratory gas exchange. Parenthetically it should be recalled that I had contacted that resident at 11:00 P.M. on day three. Between 1:00 A.M. and 2:00 A.M. on day four, the resident on call was informed by

Meyer Sonis M.D.

phone of my wife's continued poor respiratory gas exchange and the resident responded verbally by ordering increased oxygen input pressure. At 2:00 A.M. on day four, a pulmonary consultation was requested of the pulmonary service by the resident on call (parenthetically, the physician order record showed that this written order for pulmonary consultation was an insert add on to the already written orders for that time) but was not submitted to the consultant until 6:15 A.M. on day four. Between 2:00 A.M. and 3:00 A.M. on day four, the computer log indicated a precipitous drop in blood pressure, as well as an increase in respiratory rate, and the nurse's notes reported cyanosis (turning blue due to oxygen lack), decreased breath sounds in the right lobe of the lung and rhonchi (type of sound) throughout. At 5:15 A.M. on day four, blood respiratory gas results continued to be reported as poor and the resident gave a verbal order to increase the oxygen input pressure. The nurse's notes also indicated that the resident on call did not personally attend my wife during this unfolding crisis.]

As matters settled down on day four, my sons and I informed both the surgeon and the cardiologist of the events which had transpired between us and the resident on call during day three and then between us and the on-call cardiologist on day three regarding our concern about pneumonia. We indicated to the surgeon: our anger about the resident's lack of responsiveness to our suggestions; our concern with the inability of the resident to call for help and inform her superiors; and our continued apprehension regarding her judgment if she were to continue on-call coverage to my wife. The surgeon responded that he would call this to the resident's attention, and note it on her records. From then on, he would request the chief resident of the cardio-thoracic surgery department to be available to us in overseeing this resident's performance.

From day four to day fourteen (the day of my wife's death) the die seemed to have been cast by the events of day one to day four. Despite a few days of fluctuating responsiveness and

Skeletons in the Medical Closet
A Personal Story and a Professional Report

moments of metabolic normality, Anne lapsed into coma with very rudimentary brain reflexes remaining. Sequentially she deteriorated from the failure of multiple organs of her body until death. At one point twelve different medical consultants followed her medical care. My sons and I had to ask the surgeon about having one physician to coordinate her care, since the surgeon was not always available to do so, and since this Intensive Care Unit did not have a full or even part-time critical care specialist available.

On day fourteen at 3:00 A.M., my daughter and I had one hour to bid farewell to Anne as her monitors clicked off her ebbing life. Even as I write this, almost ten years later, I find myself hurting at the memory of saying goodbye to my wife. I recall now, as vividly as then, my signing of the agreement for an autopsy but with my hand written comment on the consent form indicating my proviso for conducting an autopsy, namely, my request for a copy of the total autopsy report because of my continued puzzlement as to the cause of Anne's death. In other words, the operation was successful but the patient died.

Postscript to Anne's Hospitalization

Following Anne's death, I formally requested that the hospital send me a copy of my wife's hospitalization records, including the autopsy report. Ordinarily my request of hospital reports on family members is not unusual. During my career as a physician, I have always secured copies of hospital records, medical reports and studies on members of my family. I have done so in order to abstract key findings for submission to the physicians of a family member, since many physicians may not take the time to seek out and review such records or reports. In this way, and without becoming my family's physician, I could aid my family to secure continuity in the care rendered them by their physicians. In my wife's case during her hospitalization, my sons and I did not read her record because of our belief in the long held principle of the medical profession, namely, that a physician should not become a practicing physician to his own family since his judgement might be influenced by personal feelings. Instead we shared our questions and concerns with my wife's physicians in the belief that her physicians would responsibly respond.

In requesting my wife's hospital record I had assumed that I would have no difficulty in securing these records. I had assumed that the hospital and its physicians were as concerned and puzzled about my wife's death as I was. I had assumed that I would have the help of the physicians, who cared for my wife during her hospitalization, in seeking answers. Unfortunately, all of my assumptions proved to be incorrect. In securing the hospital records, I encountered delays, road blocks, and partial responses to my inquiries about finding of errors in the 800 page record or in finding "poor" copies of material, or about missing reports. For example, on my discovery of incomplete reports on x-rays, I ultimately had to personally visit the record room of the Department of Radiology in order to secure the items requested. On one of my visits to the record room of the Department of Radiology, months after my wife's death, the record room librarian gave me a report of an x-ray of my wife taken during her last hospitalization, but which was read and transcribed three months after my wife's death because it had been misplaced into another patient's file. When I asked about discrepancies between the autopsy report and documented clinical findings in the record I received no reply. Ultimately, I discovered from an internal source at the hospital that the cause of delay in my securing the record was that the Risk Management Committee (a hospital committee whose purpose is to monitor and review the occurrence of events which have placed a patient at risk) had been reviewing the records. Further, I learned from an internal source at the hospital that there had been an internal formal report by the quality control program of the hospital on its review of my wife's record. Because of the problems I was

Skeletons in the Medical Closet
A Personal Story and a Professional Report

encountering in securing reports, it seemed to me that the hospital may have drawn the wagons around itself in a circle for defense of an action which, at that time, I had not planned nor taken. It was my belief that the hospital may have concluded internally that they were vulnerable to a legal suit and would voluntarily reveal nothing until forced to do so.

After my sons and I had independently reviewed the 800 pages of my wife's hospital record, and through a most careful cross reference of dates/ times/ nurse's notes/ laboratory studies, we were able to document the validity of the concerns which we had shared with her physicians during the initial four days of my wife's hospitalization. Our review also raised other questions. However, because of the possible but understandable personal bias in our own review of these records, we secured the services of two well respected specialist physicians, residing outside of Pittsburgh (a critical care specialist and a pulmonologist), who were prepared for a fee to serve as independent record review consultants, but with an agreement that each of them would not participate in any court proceedings if such were instituted by me. Each of them reviewed the entire hospital record and rendered their written opinions on the questions we had posed and on the nature of the medical care rendered to my wife. These consultants confirmed the validity of our concerns and produced additional findings in the record beyond those we had found.

The first of the findings was that of my wife's serious loss of blood and fluid due to the continued "oozing" from her chest tubes (placed there at surgery for drainage from the heart repair) during the first and second day post surgery. Consequent to this serious loss of fluid volume, which had to be replaced by transfusions and intravenous fluid, the laboratory report in the hospital record reported the presence of a hemorrhagic anemia, which negatively impacted on her ability to adequately oxygenate herself. In addition, there was a laboratory report in the record of an abnormal bleeding time prior to surgery, but which was not followed up by more extensive hematological studies during the period of her "oozing."

The second of the findings was that of the increasing signs of respiratory distress which was shown by my wife during days two and three post surgery. [The hospital record revealed nurse's notes and reports of abnormal blood gas exchange, but no actions on the part of the medical staff to undertake comprehensive studies, including consultation from a pulmonologist, to search out the source for this respiratory distress.]

The third finding was the delay in the timely diagnosis and appropriate treatment of the "pneumonic" infection which my wife was manifesting by signs and symptoms during day two and three post surgery. [The hospital record revealed nurse's notes regarding sputum changes, slightly elevated temperature and breathing problems which were occurring on day two and day three. There were also laboratory reports of an increase in white blood cells (a sign of infection) and abnormal blood gas readings. There was no record of a timely response by a physician for more intensive studies until late on day three and even then the studies performed ignored a vital test of the sputum. Further there was no record of treatment for the infection until the early morning of day four and even then the dosage of the antibiotic was not correct.]

The fourth finding was the delay in the timely recognition and appropriate treatment of the septic shock condition of my wife which she manifested during the early morning hours of post surgery day four, consequent to her pneumonic infection which had become overwhelming in light of the delay in initiating the correct treatment. [The hospital record revealed that her first dose of an antibiotic was administered at 1:00 A.M. on day four and that at 2:00 A.M. she began manifesting signs and symptoms of septic shock, such as a precipitous drop in blood pressure/abnormal blood gases/labored breathing/cyanosis. The nurse's notes revealed verbal communications between the nurse and physician regarding the crisis, but the record showed

Skeletons in the Medical Closet
A Personal Story and a Professional Report

no bedside direct response of the physician to this crisis. The record also revealed that during this crisis, diuretic medication (to increase fluid excretion) had been continued despite the need to stop fluid loss.]The last of the findings pertained to the emergency actions of her physicians which were required to halt and remediate the serious life threatening crisis which they encountered on day four at 6:00 A.M., but which crisis they had not known about from the resident on call during this weekend.

Based on their findings and expert experience, both physicians independently of each other had reached a conclusion that my wife's medical care during the initial four days of her hospitalization had been below established practice standards for the diagnosis and treatment of her nosocomial pneumonia (a hospital acquired infection). Though these consultants believed that my wife's chance for survival might have been increased if she had received a more timely diagnosis and appropriate treatment, they also noted that this could become a debatable issue in a court of law.

One of these physicians did make several suggestions. First, he believed that the findings in the hospital record could be strengthened by seeking and securing information in possession of the hospital about: the steps taken by and results of the hospital's search for the source of my wife's nosocomial infection; the results of any internal investigations by the hospital regarding my wife's death, such as by the Risk Management Committee, Quality Control Program, Infections Disease Committee (See Chapter on Hospitals); the reports on my wife's death which were filed by the hospital with the appropriate authorities; reports of the Peer Review Organization of the Medicare Program (See Chapter on Doctor Watchers) on their review of my wife's hospitalization record; reports of any past malpractice suits or infractions of practice patterns by the surgeon and the resident in question. An additional suggestion made by this consultant was to call the matter of the circumstances of my wife's death to the attention of the Inspector

General of the Medicare Program, and on the basis of my allegations that my wife and the Medicare Program as co-payors did not receive the standard of care they were paying for. On this latter suggestion this physician, though clearly not willing to participate as a witness in an individual legal action, was ready and willing to serve as an expert witness if a class action suit were pursued to penetrate the wall which enabled hospitals to "hide" information from the patient about their care. [Parenthetically it should be noted that this viewpoint, expressed by the physician in 1989, has become prophetic of the class action suits which led to the "hidden" information of tobacco industries, pharmaceutical companies, toxic waste dumping of industries, medical devices industry (silicon implants).]

Pursuant to: the reports of these physicians who had sent me their opinions; my lack of success in fostering communication with the hospital and surgeon; my own research into the published medical literature of pertinence to my wife's death and into the published legal literature regarding medical malpractice, I came to the conclusion that legal action may be the only avenue available to me in order to secure the answers I sought. Thus, I now sought legal consultation from two well respected legal firms, and to which I submitted a copy of my wife's hospital record, the written opinions of the two consultant physicians, my own annotations of the hospital record, references to pertinent published literature and a draft copy of a letter to the Inspector General (Medicare Program).

Legal Action

In response to my inquiry one of the legal firms replied as I have abstracted to follow: "It should be appreciated in any assessment of Mrs. Sonis' care that it is only in retrospect that we know she succumbed to lung abscesses populated by pseudomonas aeruginosa, a post-operative nosocomial complication with such a uniformly dismal outcome, despite therapy, that entertaining a malpractice suit is precluded under the circumstances. <u>Prospectively</u>, the physicians who cared for Mrs. Sonis did not have this information nor, interestingly, did they seek to obtain it but, apparently, wrote her off without any justification for having done so. It is the prospective care and its inadequacy that should be the concern of any peer review organization evaluating proper patient care and intervention, as had she not had this particular complication but merely a pneumonia, she may very well have succumbed to a similar outcome as would any patient so inadequately treated. It is for this reason that the circumstances of her death should demand critical analysis if adequate patient care is to be insured at an institution licensed by Medicare to perform specialized cardiothoracic surgery."

The other firm responded by indicating its willingness to undertake legal action on my behalf for the wrongful death of my wife, and under a recent ruling of the court in Pennsylvania that a hospital could be sued if it could be proven that the patient's chance of survival was decreased by the action(s) or lack of action(s) of the hospital and its agents. In this firm's willingness to undertake this legal action, they believed that the information in the hospital record would provide a "strong" case.

Thus I initiated two steps. First I instituted legal action against the hospital and surgeon one year after my wife's death. Secondly, I decided to submit a complaint to the Inspector General's Office of the Health Care Financing Administration (Medicare).

In taking the second step, I submitted a letter to the Inspector General which informed him of my action in suing the hospital for the alleged wrongful death of my wife. I also indicated that the information available in my wife's hospital record would support and document my allegations, and for this reason I believed that the medical care received by my wife (and for which she and medicare as copayors paid the hospital $128,000) was below the standards of practice established. This communication had a "life" all of its own. It took one year before I received a formal acknowledgement that my letter to the Inspector General had been received. For a while letters were bouncing around from one component of Medicare to another. Then a Catch 22 scenario of back and forth with the designated Peer Review Organization, ending on their letter to me indicating that, since my request for an in depth review of the hospital record by the P.R.O. (based on the information I had) was not within the scope of their current "work contract" with Medicare, perhaps I would be prepared to draft a proposal for such a review of records for consideration by the P.R.O. in their next "contract" discussions with Medicare. In short after five years I gave up and came to the conclusion that it would take a great deal more to "wake" them up to pay more attention to the shoddy medical care for which Medicare had paid.

In taking the first step, namely legal action, I have learned a great deal about the legal process, legal practice, and legal practitioners. Some of my lessons have been painful, while some of my lessons have corroborated the validity of current jokes about lawyers and judges. The legal process is slow, full of starts and stops, fraught with appointments made and changed with minimum concern or apology to the client. It is a process totally controlled by the time table and vagaries of the legal practitioners and subservient to the arrogance of these practitioners. Very little attention is paid to the needs of the client. Though I had mixed feelings about this "legal process" it ultimately became clear to me that, at the present time in the real world of seeking answers to a "wrongful death" in a hospital, the key to the answers regarding this death (if any answers are to be forthcoming from the hospital) does lie with the legal process, despite the varied objectives of the different parties involved in this process. By these varied objectives, I am referring to the fact that: the hospital is aiming, at the least cost, to protect itself from admitting to its own errors, faulty judgment of staff, and the human factors motivating actions of physicians. The doctor is aiming, at the least cost, not to be listed in the National Practitioner Data Bank (a federal law). The attorney for the hospital and doctor is aiming to fulfill the aims of the hospital and doctor, but not necessarily at the least cost of their attorney's fees, and to thwart the opposition. The attorney for the plaintiff (person suing) is aiming to thwart the hospital and doctor in their aim, but is prepared to "let them off the hook" at the highest cost to them. Finally, the family of the deceased patient is aiming to secure from the hospital and doctor as many answers to the questions they may have about the death of the patient as well as an admission of the hospital's responsibility for this death.

During the course of this legal process, I have served my attorney as a quasi-paralegal, as a quasi-medical research assistant and quasi-expert on the legal process. To serve in these roles I have performed many tasks, some of which I will briefly summarize. The tasks ranged from re-reading my wife's hospital record and annotating it further, to answering formal questionnaires (interrogatories) of the opposing attorney, to developing a file of pertinent scientific publications for my attorney, to preparing formal questionnaires (interrogatories) for submission to the opposing parties, to sitting in on depositions (formal direct verbal examination of a witness pre-trial) as a nonverbal observer. In the course of performing these various tasks, my feelings have ranged from the pain of my memories of the two week vigil at my wife's bedside to utter dismay at the prospect of securing forthright answers to questions, to sheer anger at the lackadaisical attitude of the surgeon during his deposition, to absolute disbelief in the cold and deliberate lack of recall by the resident in question during her deposition.

In my pursuit of this legal action against the hospital and surgeon, I became very conscious of the point in law which governs the legal process, namely, that the party being accused (i.e., the hospital and surgeon) is innocent of the claim made by the party (i.e., me) making the accusation until proven otherwise. Thus the object of the legal process was to provide a "level playing field" for the two parties, so that at the final moment of truth at a jury trial each party will have an equal chance to prove their "truth." This level playing field is developed during the legal process of discovery for each party through formal questionnaires (interrogatories) to each party, through formal questioning under oath (depositions) by each party of persons deposed, through providing each party with information requested by each party unless this information is privileged by attorney-client relationship. The purpose of the legal process, at least theoretically, seemed to be that the parties suing and being sued should each show all of their "cards" to the other so that each has an equal chance to prove their truth. Unfortunately I learned that this was a myth.

I have participated in answering almost two hundred questions (interrogatories) posed by the attorney for the hospital and surgeon. Questions which ranged from eliciting facts to eliciting descriptions, including questions about our income. In my development of questions for the interrogatories to be submitted to the opposing party by my attorney, I had suggested a series of questions which, if answered, could be helpful in confirming the events of the initial few days of my wife's hospitalization. Questions about the hospital and its system of management? Questions about the surgery performed? Questions to elicit information about the "sloppiness of their care," and the internal structure of the hospital which governs quality assurance? Most of these questions were not utilized by my attorney, because of his insistence that we would utilize them during the jury trial (which never took place.). More importantly, in light of the "theory" of a level playing field for all parties, it is ironic to note the general tenor of the responses to our interrogations by the opposing attorney was one of denying every allegation made until we would supply proof of such. For examples, they denied the allegations against the surgeon on the grounds that he was not responsible for what happened since he was not on call and was not informed about my wife's crisis. Even though the

Skeletons in the Medical Closet
A Personal Story and a Professional Report

surgeon was the physician responsible for my wife's care, and for which he was paid a fee, he claimed no responsibility because of his absence.

I have participated in my own deposition by the defense attorneys. Some of the questions raised were a direct outgrowth of my answers to their interrogatories; some of the questions were aimed at elaboration of comments I made regarding the critical events of the initial four days of my wife's hospitalization. Some of the questions were attempts at eliciting discrepancies in my testimony and in my answers to interrogatories; some of the questions were downright hostile. Many of the questions, directly and indirectly, focused on the discussion my sons had had with the house physician (resident in question), the reasons we did not go "over the head" of this resident, and on the discussions my sons and I had with the surgeon following the septic shock crisis. Perhaps the most hostile and painful question was posed by the hospital attorney as he attempted to place the responsibility for what happened to my wife on my sons and I because we did not go over the resident's head. He attempted to downplay or neutralize my wife's loss to me by assuming I had remarried in light of the marriage ring he saw on my finger. [Interestingly enough, this attorney apologized to me through my attorney for his hostile comment.]

I participated at the request of my attorney, as a silent observer, in the deposition of the surgeon and resident in question. It had been my hope that the surgeon could be confronted by the facts in the hospital record of my wife. Facts which could document the extent to which the surgeon was not on top of the myriad details of my wife's care and which could undermine the surgeon's denial of responsibility for the actions of his residents while he was receiving payment for his total care of my wife. My view of this deposition of the surgeon was that it did reflect his utter lack of attention to the details pertinent to my wife's care, his inability to be "on top of things" because of the volume of his surgery, his reliance or over-reliance on residents/nurses to address the post-operative care of critically ill patients.

I had hoped in the deposition of the resident in question that she could be confronted by the facts of the record which do document her delay in recognition and adequate treatment of the pneumonia and septic shock, her lack of sufficient knowledge about the specifics of my wife's situation while she (the resident) was on call and responsible for the care of 90 critically ill surgical patients.

In the deposition of the resident in question, perhaps the most revealing comment was the comment of my attorney after the deposition, namely, that in all of his years as an attorney, he has never met someone as cold, calloused and calculating as he found this resident to be during the deposition. In essence, she only responded to "neutral" questions and indicated that she could not remember the more "controversial" and possibly "damaging" events. However: she did contradict the surgeon by stating he was her Director of Training and therefore responsible for her training; she did state that on the fateful weekend coverage of my wife, she was responsible for overseeing the care of 90 to 100 surgical patients in the hospital including the Surgical Intensive Care Unit.

With the completion of the "discovery and deposition phase" of my suit, the legal process came to the "critical point" of the legal process. This critical point, as defined in legal parlance, occurs at the time when each party (plaintiff and defense) has secured a written opinion of a neutral (no conflict of interest) medical expert witness to support or rebut the allegations made and has submitted this written opinion to the court as legal evidence. It is then, and only then, that the court names the judge who will preside at the jury trial. Because we had reached this point, namely we had secured the written opinion of an expert physician witness who unequivocally indicated that my wife's care was below standards, I now believed that I was finally on my way to my day in court, to my moment of truth for securing the information which could explain my wife's death through the cross examination of all witnesses in front of a jury.

As in the past, during this legal process, my sons and I served my attorney in a variety of ways. We reviewed all written opinions of these opposing medical experts and documented our opinions by scientific publications of others. We assumed that my attorney would utilize our findings in cross examining and rebutting the other side. For examples we pointed out that: of the four experts of the defense attorney two had serious conflicts of interest in that they were employees of the hospital and had personally served as physician caregivers to my wife; one defense expert had rendered a written opinion and report based on erroneous dates and sequences of events, as well as misquotes, from the hospital record; one defense expert had quoted results of a study/publication which totally varied from the actual conclusions of this publication.

Unfortunately my naïve belief that I was now on the way to my moment of truth did not turn out to be so. Dates were set for the jury trial selection and then canceled at the last moment; delay after delay was encountered in attempting to set dates, and all of this with no explanation to me. Because of this on and off status, I even began to question my attorney as to his commitment to and interest in the suit and belief in its validity; I even began to question my own judgment and belief in my attorney. In light of this inordinate and endless delay in setting a date for jury selection and a trial, my attorney advised me and recommended that we opt for a judge's hearing instead of a jury trial because we would have a better chance of presenting our evidence. His reasoning sounded plausible; though in hindsight I must wonder if my attorney was as naïve as I was, or if I was just stupid.

Though my attorney and I had anticipated a hastening in the pace of the legal process, this did not occur. Instead as before, dates were set and canceled over and over again. For examples: one date was set and canceled because of the admission to a hospital of the judge's mother; one date was set and cancelled at the last moment because the defense attorney had decided to undergo elective surgery; dates were unable to be set because of a seeming inability for all parties to communicate; other dates would be set and changed because the judge was unavoidably detained due to his "electioneering for higher office." [Parenthetically, and contemporaneous with the difficulty in setting a date with the judge it should be noted that an investigative report team for a local newspaper had reported on their study of "absentee" judges in Pittsburgh, including the judge assigned to my suit who had not had an "open court" for three months.]

Finally, a date for the judge's hearing was set and held, about eight years after my suit had been filed. In preparation for this hearing my attorney informed me that: the judge had allowed 1 to 1½ days for this hearing; no medical expert witnesses would testify since the judge had their written opinions; each attorney had already submitted their written briefs to the judge; I would be able to tell my story under questioning.

At the designated date and time of 9:00 A.M. my attorney and I were present in the judge's courtroom, as were the defense attorney, the risk management representative for the hospital and to my surprise one of the defense expert witnesses (who had a conflict of interest because he was an employee of the hospital and had been a medical consultant to my wife.) We were then informed by the court clerk that the hearing would start later because the judge had other court matters to attend to in his private chambers. Shortly before 10:30 A.M., at which time the hearing officially began, the judge requested a meeting in his chambers with the plaintiff and defense attorneys and the representative of the risk management of the hospital.

Before I proceed with a summary account of the hearing I must admit that I had not been prepared for the "comedy" in justice and fair play which was enacted during the hearing. Contrary to my previous information that the hearing would probably last for 1 to 1½ days, the hearing lasted one and a half hours (with frequent pauses so that the judge could attend to some court matters awaiting him in his chambers). The attorneys raised no question with the judge about these stops and starts.

During this hearing the actions, behavior and verbalizations of the judge left me with the impression that he was preoccupied with other matters, constantly in a hurry to keep things moving, harrying the lawyers with questions and interruptions, very busy taking notes during everyone's presentations, and at times had to have the attorneys restate something he had missed. At times each lawyer was so busy trying to "hurry" that they almost fell over each other, but each never raised any objection to the court's action or behavior. Parenthetically I felt sorrow for these two adult men who almost groveled at the feet of the judge. There were times when I truly could not hear the lawyers distinctly because they were facing the judge and speaking at a very fast clip. I was given my day in court, and after eight years of waiting was sworn in to give my testimony under questioning only by my attorney. My testimony was brief since I was asked to reply to three questions only, namely, my name, my relationship to the deceased, and whether I was at my wife's bedside to observe the care given her. I was then excused.

The final act to this comedy of justice and fair play occurred when the medical expert of the defense was called to the stand. No other "experts" were present. I was flabbergasted but could not talk to my attorney. Despite the apparent conflict of interest of this expert, the judge and my attorney did not question this. Nor did the judge or my attorney request proof of the validity and source of his statement that in his long experience with the hospital as their infectious disease expert, the hospital has never had this specific type of virulent organism acquired by a patient except for a report on one patient subsequent to my wife as an "index case." Further there was no mention made of this "internal" information in his previously written opinion. It was clear that he was referring to internal information which had not

Meyer Sonis M.D.

been referred to in his written opinion nor had the defense attorney made any effort to reveal this "internal" information to the plaintiff's attorney, nor did my attorney question this. Upon conclusion of the hearing, the judge requested a written statement, of no more than two or three pages, from each lawyer on their closing argument. Further the judge announced that upon his review of all material available to him he would render his opinion. At the conclusion of this hearing my lawyer felt optimistic about the outcome, despite the questions I had about the manner and process of this hearing. Two weeks after the conclusion of the hearing I spoke with my attorney regarding the status of the judge's report; he informed me that the judge had ruled in favor of the defense. On my questioning of my attorney about the basis by which the judge had arrived at his conclusion my attorney informed me that no basis had been provided. In speaking at much greater length to my attorney he clearly expressed his surprise and disappointment. He agreed with me about the irregularities which took place at the hearing, namely, the shortness of the hearing, the fact that there was no transcription of the hearing which ordinarily occurs, the use of a witness who had a conflict of interest, the defense attorney withholding information from the plaintiff's attorney. He agreed to send me a copy of the judge's decision since I never received a written notice, as well as to send me copies of material he had given the judge.

Despite my several formal requests of my attorney to send me a copy of the judge's ruling as well as a copy of the final brief of my attorney which he had submitted to the judge, I was never given the courtesy of a response. And further, despite my several formal requests of the judge for a copy of his ruling and a copy of the transcription of the hearing (if such took place), and for which copies I would defray the cost, I never received the courtesy of a response. Consequently I assumed that my attorney was wanting to wash his hands entirely of this matter and that the judge did not have any responsibility to me as the aggrieved person. At that point I too felt that enough was enough. Subsequently, but only following upon my decision to not pursue this matter any further within the legal system, I took the step of actually reviewing the "formal" record of my suit as filed in the "publicly available" prothonotary's office. To my surprise I did learn something which my attorney never told me regarding the "dropping of my allegation against the surgeon," namely that the court (prior to my attorney's recommendation to me to opt for a judge's hearing) had given my attorney three formal notices for providing the defense attorney with information requested but to which notices my attorney did not response. This led the court (also in the formal court record) to dismiss the suit against the surgeon. [Parenthetically this information was contained in the various reports and comments I had prepared for my attorney.]

In summing up my understanding of the judge's hearing, I was supposed to believe that: my wife was admitted to the hospital already "harboring this virulent organism;" my wife, under the known risk of stress of cardiac surgery, infected herself with her own virulent organism; once she had this virulent organism, which can be fatal in up to 80% of cases according to a "biased" expert, the die was cast for her fatal outcome, regardless of what was done or/and when it was done or not done.

I must note according to the published literature, that the blame the victim technique is a common tactic of a defense in personal injury suits. In my wife's case the strategy of the defense attorney: during the deposition phase was to blame my sons and me for what happened to my wife because we did not go over the head of the resident; during the judge's hearing was to blame my wife for her death because she self-infected herself, even though the defense could not prove their allegation.

Meyer Sonis M.D.

Conclusion

On my looking back at the personal story which has unfolded for me during these past ten years, there can be no doubt of the many lessons I have learned. After 45 years of companionship with my wife, I have learned to live by myself, with myself, and most important I have learned about myself. After eight years of my struggle with the legal process there also can be no doubt of the many lessons I have learned about the legal process, the tyranny of lawyers and judges, the abuse by "elected" judges of the public trust in them, the law schools and the serious criticism of their methods and outcomes; but most important I have learned about my naivete and stupidity in not being more aggressive regarding my "right" as an aggrieved person within this legal process. During this time I have amassed a great deal of information, some of which has been specific to my wife's death, some of which has been specific to the hospital in which my wife died, some of which has been general and applicable to the Skeletons I will refer to in the Medical Closet, but all of which I believe pertinent to those interested in becoming informed consumers of medical and hospital care.

As a consequence of my intense scrutiny of the questions posed by my wife's death, I have secured information about: the serious problems which nosocomial infections continue to pose for hospitalized patients as a result of laxity in hospital practices; the fact that, even in 1989, various of the leading centers for cardiac surgery in the United States had published manuals to guide others in the standards of care required to prevent and/or identify and/or treat complications of cardiac surgery, and which were not followed in my wife's situation; the increased opportunity for survival of critically ill hospitalized patients in an Intensive Care Unit through the utilization of a critical care medical specialist to direct critical care, and which did not occur in my wife's situation.

Skeletons in the Medical Closet
A Personal Story and a Professional Report

As a consequence of my intense scrutiny of the hospital in which my wife died, I have secured information about: procedures which were not performed by the hospital, but for which nevertheless bills were presented; misplaced, missing, untimely reports of laboratory and other studies; serious and uncorrected errors in reporting in the hospital record; an overscheduled and overworked house staff, with insufficient supervision by staff physicians; physician progress notes which not only do not match the clinical condition of the patients but also are recorded in violation of standards set for such reports; physicians who do not read nurses' notes; the very heavy operating room schedule of the cardiac surgeons who, in 1989 grossed charges of over 61 million dollars for the hospital, but who relied very heavily on others to monitor the care of their critically ill patients; reports of the hospital, which we could not secure during the legal process, but which registered concern of the Quality Review Program of the hospital. Perhaps more damning than other information I had secured was information (now known to the community at large) regarding the hospital system of management which produced "shoddy medical practices" and "fiscal irregularities" while expanding the greed of the hospital to the point now of bankruptcy.

As a consequence of my scrutiny of my own profession and hospital, through several studies which I personally conducted, I have found other doctors who have had adverse events occur to themselves or their families during hospitalization and who have also had similar experiences with the conspiracy of silence of the hospital. At the same time, my scrutiny has found that the quality of assurance programs in a hospital does hold out the promise of serving as a safety net for catching patients at risk before they fall through.

In concluding this personal story I must remind the reader: that the events which are described by me as occurring to my wife during her last hospitalization were not in question by the court; that the actions which were taken or not taken by the hospital as recorded in the hospital record of my wife during her last hospitalization were not in question by the court; however, that my allegations of medical negligence by the hospital in causing my wife's medical injuries and death were in question by the court as having not been proven. In other words, in the court's eyes, in this instance, the care provided by the hospital to my wife was in keeping with "their" standards of care for a patient with my wife's medical condition requiring surgery, my wife's risk vulnerability due to her past history, and the known risk factors imposed by cardiac surgery of valve replacement.

CHAPTER TWO

MEDICAL INJURIES, MEDICAL ERRORS HOSPITAL MISTAKES, MEDICAL NEGLIGENCE

In the fall of 1996 a most unusual, and perhaps a first of its kind, medical conference took place in the United States. This conference was significant for several reasons.

First of all, it's significance lay in the wide range of the co-sponsors of this conference and in the broad scope of agents participating in the conference, namely: the body politic of organized medicine and health professions; national accreditation and standard setting bodies for the health professions and hospitals; physicians, nurses, psychologists, safety engineers from the space/nuclear/airplane and transportation industries, human factor scientists and researchers, hospital managers, pharmaceutical experts. Indeed, strange bedfellows.

Second of all, its significance lay in the subject matter which the conference addressed, namely: Examining Errors in Health Care.

As a physician of some fifty plus years, I had never thought the time would come when I would live to see the body politic of organized medicine (American Medical Association) in the United States openly and publicly acknowledge the occurrence of medical errors, as well as the need for the medical and health professions to do something about this. This acknowledgment by the AMA was the proverbial shot in the arm to bring the skeletons out of the medical closet and to shatter the conspiracy of silence which has surrounded the subject of medical errors for so long.

As a consequence of the success of this medical conference, the American Medical Association in 1997 announced its formation of a National Patient Safety Foundation, which would provide an organized base for collection and dissemination of information and data about the safety of medical and health care in the United States. In 1998 the National Patient Safety Foundation announced the convening in 1998 of the second national medical conference on the subject of patient safety, medical errors, hospital mistakes.

After my review of the audio and published content of this medical conference, and after my review of published literature on the subject of medical errors and hospital mistakes, I felt it is indeed unfortunate that this wealth of information has not been made more understandable and available to the lay public. Though information about this subject has trickled down to the lay public, who are also concerned about the safety of the health care they receive, it has continued to be disseminated primarily in sound bytes, brief medical coverage, horror stories and headline news for a day or two.

To the average lay person it may seem that the occurrence of medical errors, hospital mistakes, medical negligence is a comparatively new phenomenon because of the more recent public visibility about medical errors and hospital mistakes. However, the historical record of medicine's evolution reveals that such occurrences were taking place as far back as the time of Hippocrates and the Babylonian kings. In fact in the codes of law of Babylonian kings, an injunction is made that a physician whose hands have caused harm to a patient should have his fingers amputated. In my own early days of medical practice in 1950, and in the decades preceding, many physicians and health related professionals knew about the occurrence of medical injuries, but these occurrences received little or no public visibility because of the "conspiracy of silence" which was maintained by physicians and others. Despite this conspiracy of silence, a phrase was coined to describe the occurrence of a medical injury as an iatrogenic (doctor caused) injury to a patient during their medical care (in or out of a hospital). This term of iatrogenic injury became an all inclusive term for medical errors, hospital mistakes, medical negligence, medical malpractice, medical misadventures, therapeutic misadventures. A commentary about how things have changed is born out by an article written by a physician for recent publication in the New Yorker on *How Doctors Make Mistakes.* Such an article would never have seen the light of day as recently as twenty-five years ago.

With the increased pressure on the medical profession and health providers, during the period of 1970 to the present, for them to assume greater accountability for the safety, competence and quality of care which they render to the public, clinical scientists had begun to delve more seriously into the issues and problems of medical errors, hospital mistakes, medical negligence, medical malpractice. In the early 70's the field of anesthesiology became a pioneer in the attention which they gave to addressing the very high rate of patient deaths due to anesthesia. In the early 80's various scientific studies began to yield data and information of a more reliable nature about medical malpractice claims, medical errors, hospital mistakes. Though seminal studies had been performed during the past thirty years perhaps the most promising of such studies were those conducted and initially reported by the Harvard Medical Practice Study Group in 1989. These initial studies have become a paradigm for investigating and understanding medical errors, hospital mistakes, medical negligence and medical malpractice. These scientifically and statistically designed studies were based on a review of 31,000 medical records of hospitalized patients selected on a random sample basis from a population of 2.5 million patients discharged from 51 different hospitals in New York in 1984. These studies were designed to provide quantitative data and qualitative information about: the extent (incidence) of patient injuries resulting from medical intervention during hospitalization; the extent to which these injuries were due to negligence; the extent to which these injuries (negligent and non-negligent) were preventable; the extent to which these injuries led to litigation; the extent of economic loss caused by these injuries and the extent of compensation for these injuries.

Adverse Events: Medical Injuries

With the expansion of/in our knowledge about medical injuries occurring to hospitalized patients, the term of iatrogenic injuries was supplanted by the more meaningful term of Adverse Events. An Adverse Event (AE) was defined as an unintended, unplanned for, unanticipated incident or event which occurred to a hospitalized patient and can: lead to an injury or disability of minor or major catastrophic proportions (death); produce problems for the patient beyond the medical complications usually associated with the medical condition for which the patient sought medical care; prolong the length of stay for the patient in the hospital. The presence of an Adverse Event (AE) does not necessarily signify poor medical care nor does its absence signify good medical care. Rather the presence of an AE can signal the possibility that a medical error or hospital mistake has taken place. Thus the AE serves as a marker of a possible "bad thing" happening to a patient during their medical and hospital care.

It could be of tremendous help, in alerting us to the possible "bad things" which can occur to patients during the process of receiving medical and hospital care, if we had an exhaustive and comprehensive list of all possible adverse events which can befall a patient. Unfortunately a list is eminently improbable because of the manner by which adverse events are usually brought to light. I am referring to the fact that adverse events, which can produce medical errors or hospital mistakes, are usually made known through the self reporting of an incident by a caregiver, reporting of such by quality control or risk management programs of the hospital, "internal" gossip in the hospital. For these reasons, among others, there is a tendency for an under reporting of such events. Therefore, short of mandating an autopsy on every patient who dies in a hospital, we must rely on studies, reports and conferences such as referred to in this chapter for more reliable estimates regarding the extent to which adverse events may be happening to the general population of patients.

For the purpose of providing the lay reader with a sample of incidents or events which can signal the occurrence of an adverse event to a hospitalized patient several examples follow. These are the kind of events which were utilized by the Harvard Study Group in their screening of medical records for potential medical errors. It is also these kind of events which were highlighted by me in my telling of my personal story. Among such events are, but to mention a few: the unanticipated death of a patient during hospitalization; the development by the hospitalized patient of an infection; the presence of a wound infection following surgery; the return to the operating room of a patient following surgery; the transfer of a hospitalized patient from acute general medical care to intensive care; the readmission of a patient to a hospital shortly after discharge from a hospital; the falling out of bed of an elderly hospitalized patient; the development of cardiac or respiratory arrest of a hospitalized patient; an elevated temperature in a hospitalized patient, on the day before or on the day of discharge; an unfavorable drug reaction of a hospitalized patient; the development of organ damage in the hospitalized patient following an invasive procedure; indication in the medical record of litigation by a hospitalized patient.

Without going into the details of the various published studies and reports which are now available regarding adverse events, it can be said that the findings of such studies have significantly advanced our knowledge about medical injuries. Rather I will provide a "sample" of the results of such studies and cite references of these studies in the references (appendix). Because the studies of the Harvard Study Group achieved a "gold standard" in the reliability of their data, I will focus my comments on the data of their studies.

It is estimated that approximately 4% of all hospitalized patients, or 1.3 million of the (1990) estimated 22 million people hospitalized annually, experience an AE. Though 72% of these AE's were estimated not to be due to medical negligence, an appalling 28% however were estimated as due to medical negligence. Thus, at a national level of the 1.3 million suffering an AE: 360 thousand of these hospitalized patients would suffer an AE causing medical injury due to medical negligence; 120 thousand would suffer an AE causing medical injury so serious as to cause death. As one of the investigators of the Harvard Group remarked at the national conference (referred to earlier), "the number of hospitalized patients who die as a consequence of a medical injury could be equated with the crash of a jumbo jet killing 300 passengers every other day for one year." The investigator believed that if this happened the outcry of the public would demand change in the airline industry.

The distinction between a medical injury which is deemed due to medical negligence as contrasted with one that is not is based on the judgment that the medical care rendered was below the standards of medical practice established for the diagnosis and treatment of the specific medical injury suffered. This is basically a judgment call on the part of the parties or party responsible for the call, whether they are physicians or judges or a hospital committee or an insurance company. Because this is a judgement call there can be different opinions between parties making this judgment call. This should not be surprising in light of the uncertainty of our medical knowledge and the complicated nature of clinical decision making. For purpose of illustration several examples follow.

A non-negligent medical injury is one in which a hospitalized patient suffers a stroke following upon an angioplasty, but which procedure was judged to have been indicated by the standards established for the treatment of coronary artery disease and was performed in keeping with standards established for this procedure and with a stroke known to occur as a risk of this procedure. A negligent medical injury (AE) is one in which an elderly hospitalized patient falls out of bed twice and who dies as a consequence of the medical injury suffered. A negligent medical injury is one of a 50 year old man who is hospitalized for treatment of prostate cancer but following surgery develops a wound infection with massive bleeding requiring a return to surgery.

From the Harvard Group studies, as well as from other studies, it is estimated that about one third (33%) of medical injuries whether negligent or not were occurring to hospitalized patients who were 65 years of age or older. In fact, elderly hospitalized patients ran double the risk of a medical injury taking place over hospitalized middle aged patients. This is what could be expected in light of the fact that elderly persons tend to be more chronically ill and manifest more complicated medical problems requiring more hospitalizations and procedures than younger aged patients. For this reason physicians and hospitals need to be more alert to the possibility of adverse events occurring to the elderly hospitalized population.

Of interest in the data from these studies, because of its implications for the prevention, diagnosis and treatment of medical injuries, 50% of these injuries occurred and were identified during the same hospitalization. This suggests that for a good number of hospitalized patients who suffer a medical injury it may be possible to catch them in the "safety net programs" of a hospital and offer them timely help. In a subsequent chapter labeled "The Hospital Industry," I will provide more details about these monitoring systems and their potential to serve as a "safety net."

Ordinarily it is difficult to find reliable data on the extent to which medical injuries may be taking place in the physician's office, and/or in outpatient care and/or in nursing homes. The Harvard Group study shed some light on this in that 20% of the medical injuries found in the hospital records reviewed had occurred in the physician's office but were discovered during the subsequent hospitalization of the patient. In a study of autopsies over a ten year period of time, a county coroner (Pittsburgh) reported 63 fatal "therapeutic misadventures" of which 92% occurred in hospitals, 4% in nursing homes, 4% in physician's office.

Most hospitalized patients do receive medical care which is safe, competent and meet the standards established. Most adverse events occurring to hospitalized patients, as reported in the literature, result in medical injuries which are of minor consequence and are fully recoverable. Unfortunately, however, some of these medical injuries result in permanent impairment and disability or death. It is estimated that 60% of medical injuries produce minimal impairment and 15% result in permanent disability or death. From data available it would seem that the more serious the medical injury, such as death, the greater likelihood it is due to negligence.

Medical injuries can also be characterized according to the type (surgical or non-surgical), the setting where the injuries occurred (in the hospital, outside the hospital), the medical specialty which was involved in the injury. On the matter of type, about 50% of medical injuries were surgical, and 50% were non-surgical. Of the surgical type of medical injuries, the largest percentage was that due to a failure of surgery (36%), followed by wound infections (14%); of the non-surgical type of medical injury the largest percentage was that due to adverse drug events (20%) followed by diagnostic (8%), and therapeutic mishaps (8%). Of interest it should be noted that of all medical injuries which were due to negligence it was found that 17% were surgical in origin, while 37% were non-surgical in origin (75% of these were due to diagnostic mishap). Because of the importance of these findings, a section in this chapter will be found on ADE (Adverse Drug Events) and a section on errors and failures.

Of the settings in which the medical injuries had occurred 81% happened in the hospital (as in operating room, patient's room, Intensive Care Unit), 14% happened outside the hospital (physician's office, outpatient care). As would be expected: 41%

of medical injuries in hospitals took place in the operating room and only 2% in the x-ray room while 8% of the out of hospital medical injuries took place in a doctor's office. Of these various settings in which the negligent medical injuries occurred 70% took place in the emergency room of the hospital or in the x-ray room while 24% took place in the outpatient setting.

Of the various medical and surgical specialties involved in medical injuries, the highest rate was found in vascular surgery, thoracic and cardiac surgery and neuro-surgery, while the largest percentage of negligent medical injuries were found in obstetrics, general medicine and general surgery.

Adverse Drug Reaction (ADR): Adverse Drug Events (ADE)

An Adverse Drug Reaction is a more limited term than an Adverse Drug Event. It denotes a reaction of a patient (in or out of a hospital) to the medication taken, and usually manifests itself as one of the side effects known to occur with a drug or as an allergic reaction to a drug (hypersensitivity). An Adverse Drug Event (ADE), however, is a much broader term which has only come into prominence more recently. The ADE denotes a medical injury due to an ADR or due to an error in the prescription, manufacture, preparation, administration of medications. For example, an ADE can include: a reaction of the patient to the medication, such as a penicillin side effect; a prescription for medication which is contraindicated, such as ordering penicillin for a patient with a known reaction to penicillin; a prescription for medication which should not be given with other medications taken by the patient; a prescription for medication with the wrong dosage; the misreading of a prescription by the pharmacist preparing the medication; the inclusion of the wrong ingredients by the preparer of the medication; the inadequate quality control of a medication by the manufacturer of the medication; the error in dosage or site of an injection or timing of medication by the person administering the medication; lack of adequate monitoring of medications by the responsible party or program for such in the hospital. A potential ADE is denoted as a "near miss" in that an ADE was avoided by earlier identification in the chain (prescribing, manufacture, preparing, dispensing) prior to actual taking of the medication.

As with Adverse Events themselves, hard and reliable data about Adverse Drug Events have been difficult to come by and for very similar reasons, namely: the dependence on self reports by the perpetrator of the event; the association of "blame" on the party involved which supports denial or non-reporting; the utilization of medical records in order to retrospectively collect data but which records may have been "sanitized."

However, and fortunately, during the period of 1990 to the present more reliable data about ADE's has been generated by the design of more sophisticated and scientifically based studies and reports. For purposes of this chapter, the data and information reported has been aggregated so it can be more understandable to the lay reader. Before proceeding I do want to note that one of these studies of ADE's, conducted by the Harvard Group, has become the "gold standard" for such studies because of the prospective nature of their study of hospitalized patients (i.e. gathering data *during* the patient's stay in the hospital).

From these studies and reports it has become rather clear that ADE's are a common occurrence to hospitalized patients and that the probability is great that they are still under reported. The adverse drug event rates for hospitalized patients vary depending on the type of study performed, ranging from less than 1% for self report studies, or for population record review studies, to 4% for computerized screening studies, to 6.5% for chart (medical record) review and report studies, to 10% for combined chart review and computerized screening. Extrapolating this data to the general population of hospital admissions, medical injuries or

Skeletons in the Medical Closet
A Personal Story and a Professional Report

Adverse Events occur to 1.3 million patients annually, of which 260,000 such patients suffer an ADE.

In one study it was reported that of all of the ADE's occurring to hospitalized patients almost 30% were deemed or judged as preventable, while 1% were deemed fatal, 12% life threatening, 30% serious, and 57% significant. For every preventable ADE, it is estimated that there are three times as many potential preventable ADE's. Errors which ultimately produced an ADE were most frequently occurring at the stage of ordering (physician caused, 49%) and least in the stage of transcription (writing of prescription, 11%). The most common error by a physician was made on ordering of a drug with a wrong dose, followed decreasingly by wrong choice, prescribing allergic medication to a patient known to be allergic to the medication.

In another study into ADE's it was reported that patients over 60 years of age suffered such an event 2.5 times more frequently than those under 60. This is not surprising since the elderly tend to utilize more medications than others because of their more complicated medical conditions, and thus they run the greater risk of an ADE. More ADE's occurred to patients in the intensive care unit of the hospital than in the general care units. Of importance in this study was the fact that by using a computerized system for monitoring the detection and characteristics of ADE, the hospital increased detection sixty fold.

In a 1995 study on the appropriateness of prescribing anti-epileptic medication, it was found that only a quarter of the patients were found to be at the appropriate blood levels suggesting that the physician dosage was incorrect. A conclusion of that study was the likelihood that correcting such a problem might result in substantial cost reduction and improving clinical results.

In a most interesting study of the utilization of an automated dose checker to serve as a monitoring device to check on the dose of drugs being prescribed and to generate an alert for dosage correction, it was found that out of 29,000 drug orders, dosage problems were found in 10% of these orders (i.e. an overdose in 70% and an under dose in 30%.) In yet another study of the accuracy in preparing intravenous solutions, it was reported that an error rate occurred of 10% and with the wrong dosage found as the most common type of error. In a most revealing study, which was reported in the first national conference on medical errors referred to earlier, the investigators described the results of their survey of the perception of the physician himself/herself regarding the causes of medication prescribing errors, namely that 17% of physicians attributed the error to their lack of knowledge about the medication, while 42% attributed it to a simple "mental slip," and 39% blamed the error on others.

Finally, in a revealing study (1994) to examine the extent of inappropriate drug prescribing for patients 65 years of age or older living in the community, it was reported that approximately a quarter of the elderly received at least one of 20 drugs which were contraindicated for them and thus were placed at risk for an ADE. Inappropriateness in this study was defined as medications which should be entirely avoided, excessive dosage of medication, excessive duration of continuing the medication. The medications most commonly abused were sedatives, anti-depressants, anti-hypertensives and analgesics.

In summing up the information on of the occurrence of Adverse Drug Events or potential Adverse Drug Events to hospitalized patients, it becomes very clear that: such events are a significant problem for a hospitalized patient, as well as for patients receiving medication while in other settings; the system for monitoring of such ADE possibilities in a hospital leaves much to be desired; the behavior of physicians regarding these medication problems requires modification.

Skeletons in the Medical Closet
A Personal Story and a Professional Report

Medical Errors

There is no doubt of the fact that the occurrence of medical injuries to hospitalized patients is a much more common event than had previously been suspected. There also is no doubt that these medical injuries are probably taking place more frequently than has been reported or recorded. There can be no doubt that medical negligence is a more frequent cause of these medical injuries than previously believed. Finally there is no doubt that medical errors in medical practice do occur and in a measure never before suspected. Before proceeding with any further amplification of medical errors, several factors must be noted.

To begin with, not all medical errors can be judged as due to medical negligence. Some medical errors occur because the action of a physician is based on the as yet uncertain knowledge about diseases/illnesses and their diagnoses and most effective treatment so that the doctor is having to make a decision about doing or not doing something. Some medical errors occur because the action of a physician is based on faulty or inadequate knowledge which is not in keeping with the standards of medical care established for the diagnosis, treatment, management of a patient's specific medical condition. Medical errors which are due to medical negligence, and result in medical injuries to a patient, have medico-legal implications. Some examples of negligent medical errors have been previously given. Additional examples of such are: the lack of action of a physician to explore the symptom of rectal bleeding in a patient; the overlooked surgical sponge in the abdomen of a patient undergoing surgery; the lack of attention to abnormal laboratory findings in a compromised patient.

Secondly, and as will be expanded on at greater length in the chapter to follow, it must be remembered that medical errors may not be totally eliminated in medical practice because of the human factors involved and the management system in which medical practice takes place.

Meyer Sonis M.D.

Based on their review of 30,000 medical records of discharged hospitalized patients, the Harvard Study Group (referred to earlier) were able to cull out from these records the errors which were judged to be the cause of the medical injury. From this list they were able to develop categories and sub-categories into which the identified errors fell. Without going into the details of the data and information generated but with reference to this data annotations in the appendix, I will provide a "sampling" which I believe can be of value to the lay reader.

Five major categories were delineated. The first was that of medical injuries caused by the <u>performance</u> of a physician in doing a procedure or the lack of performance in doing a medical procedure. Examples of such errors of performance or lack of performance are: a technical error in the course of conducting/ doing the procedure; inadequate monitoring of the patient following a procedure; the utilization by the physician of an inappropriate procedure.

The second category was that of a physician error in <u>preventing</u> a medical injury. Examples of such errors were: an avoidable delay in initiating treatment or correction of the medical condition of the patient; a physician failure to utilize or order tests which are known to be indicated in the case of a given medical condition. A third category of medical error was that of an error in the <u>diagnoses</u> of a patient's medical condition. Examples of such errors were: the failure of a physician to utilize indicated tests; the failure of a physician to act on the results of tests ordered or findings of medical studies. Other categories of medical errors which cause medical injuries were: drug treatment errors; errors of commission or omission; system management problems of the hospital itself, such as failure of equipment, inadequate training of personnel in the appropriate use of equipment, insufficient or inadequate opportunity for the "medical team" to communicate with each other, "sloppy" supervision and monitoring of patient care.

Skeletons in the Medical Closet
A Personal Story and a Professional Report

Of the various categories of errors in their samples the Harvard group noted that 70% of all medical injuries were preventable in their judgment, 35% were due to performance errors while 3% were due to system management errors, Of the performance errors 38% were judged as due to negligence while in the system management errors 66% were judged as due to negligence. Of interest to note were the findings that of all categories and subcategories of errors 44% were due to technical errors but only 20% of these were deemed as negligent errors, while 17% were due to errors in diagnosis but 71% of these were deemed negligent. Other startling findings were those regarding the utilization of indicated testing in elderly patients who were diabetic: only 16% had testing for assessing extent of sugar in the hemoglobin; only 40% had retinal examination and only 55% had their cholesterol measured, in light of the fact that eye and cardiac complications are often found in elderly diabetics.

In a study of medical errors which produce medical injuries, the authors suggested that with the continued growth and expansion of new technologies and procedures, medications, interventions in the care of hospitalized patients, the system management of the hospital will become more complex and thus more vulnerable to system errors with tragic consequences.

In a study of almost 10,000 surgical malpractice claims of negligence (which used the insurance investigative data) it was reported that 35% of these "surgical misadventures" were due to improperly performed procedures, 14% to errors in diagnosis, 1% to surgery of the wrong patient or body part. Of all medico-legal claims of negligence of physicians, the delayed diagnosis of breast cancer was reported as the most serious.

In a study conducted along similar lines as in the Harvard Study group and reported on in Australia the investigators examined the medical records of hospitalized patients in 28 different hospitals. They found that 16% of these patients suffered an adverse event due to a health care worker error, wherein 50% of these medical injuries were minor, 30% of these injuries led to disability for up to a year, 20% of these injuries led to varying degrees of permanent disability/ death. This same study found that in 56% of the cases, quality assurance or peer review would have prevented the initial mistake, 11% could have been prevented by "hospital" (system) corrections. The headline reporting this study in The Sydney Morning Newspaper was, "Hospital Errors Kill 14,000 patients Per Year."

Failures In Hospitals: Failures of Hospitals

To begin with, the failures to which I am referring are not those failures in a patient's recovery which may be due to the nature of their own medical or surgical disease, illness, condition or injury and/or due to actions or behavior on their part (such as continued smoking, unsafe sex, drug and alcohol abuse) and/or due to their inability to comply with medical recommendations made (skipping medications, diet, follow-up). Rather I am referring to failures in hospitals which are a consequence of unanticipated complications in a patient's care due to human errors on the part of hospital personnel responsible for their care while hospitalized and/or due to mechanical failures in medical equipment or supplies utilized during their hospitalization and/or due to inadequacy of the hospital's system for monitoring.

In regard to these failures in hospitals or of hospitals, up until recently, reliable data was difficult to secure for a variety of reasons, not least of which were: the fear on the part of hospitals of malpractice and negligence suits; the need on the part of hospitals to avoid "bad press" for fear of losing out to the competition or jeopardizing its accreditation or certification for receiving fees from third party payors; the fear on the part of hospitals of instilling a lack of confidence in them by their patients; the silence of the hospital itself in calling attention to physicians who may be performing "shoddy" medical care.

As a consequence of a change toward greater public visibility of the failures in and of hospitals during the past decade, the nature and extent of these hospital failures has become well documented in studies and reports referred to in the previous subsections of this chapter as well as in the references (appendix). To supplement the data presented already, I will cite but a few other examples.

In 1989 the Joint Commission on Accreditation of Health Organizations (JCAHO), a national voluntary organization which accredits hospitals based on agreed upon and established standards, reported that 30% of the hospitals which the JCAHO accredited failed to meet requirements regarding standards of care, while 50% of these accredited hospitals had inadequate procedures for monitoring the outcome of surgical procedures. In another study, it was reported that in hospitals which perform 150 or fewer cardiac bypass surgery operations per year, about 10% of those patients undergoing cardiac bypass surgery for coronary disease died of complications, while only 2% or 3% died of cardiac bypass surgery complications in hospitals performing 150 or more such operations per year. Some studies have indicated that up to 20% of the cardiac bypass operations are unnecessary. Several studies have reported on the wide geographic and population class variation in rates of admissions to hospitals and surgery utilization by patients with the same diagnosis, such as differences in lengths of hospital stay, differences in number of hysterectomies (removal of uterus), and differences between lower and higher economic status. This has suggested that the differences are not random (accidental). In a study of one hospital it was estimated that for every 1000 orders for medication which were written by physicians for a hospitalized patient 3+ errors were found and with over half of these errors rated as having serious adverse consequences. In California it was recently reported that for pregnant women the higher their income the more likely it was that they would face a Cesarean section.

In our understanding of these failures in hospitals it must be emphatically noted that these failures are not a consequence of ill intent on the part of the personnel providing hospital care to a patient. Rather these failures can be the result of human errors, blunders, judgments on the part of reputable/conscientious /respected personnel serving the hospitalized patient. Therefore, as with all humans, these members of the clinical team are as prone to the human frailties, attributes, characteristics, emotions which can influence human behavior, cognitive processes, actions and judgments.

As will be detailed in the chapter to follow it is from such human factors that adverse events can occur to the hospitalized patient, as illustrated in the following examples. An error of omission or commission on the part of any member of the clinical care team because of being side tracked while preparing medication or replying to a phone call from outside of the operating room while in the process of performing surgery. A physician who is performing a risky procedure but with minimum or no experience with this procedure or under no supervision from a more experienced physician. Physicians who are impaired because of drug/alcohol abuse or illness so that this state impinges on their judgment. Physicians with insufficient time available to them for review of extensive records or discussions with or about the hospitalized patient because of the heavy schedule of patients in their patient load. The shortage of hospital personnel, due to budgetary considerations, as compared to the number required to adequately "cover" the number and kind of patients in their care.

As to the failures of hospitals which has been reported on as system management problems, I am referring to medical injuries of hospitalized patients which result from mistakes or actions which are totally under the control of the management (managers) of the hospital. Such failures of hospitals can be illustrated in the several examples to follow.

To begin with are the failures of the equipment in a hospital which may be produced by failures in the manufacture, production or preparation of medical equipment or supplies

Skeletons in the Medical Closet
A Personal Story and a Professional Report

(similar to the problems in manufacture of washing machines/dryers/television sets/automobiles/Hubble telescope), or by failures of a hospital to observe periodic and regular maintenance of equipment or by failures of hospitals to not abuse equipment (similar to abuse of household equipment) or by failures of hospitals to not replace aged equipment. There can be no doubt of the even greater importance (now and in the future) to hospitalized patients is the potential of equipment failures in light of the reliance of hospitals on high technology equipment. Thus, equipment failures of hospitals which can result in injuries to hospitalized patients because of: the reutilization of medical equipment or supplies which are designed for single use only (i.e., intravenous equipment, mouthpieces for respirators); the lack of attention to periodic recalibration of instruments as called for by the manufacturers (i.e., anesthetic machine valves, gauges, blood pressure gauges, electronic gas analyzers); the continued repairs on faulty equipment which should be replaced; a staff who are insufficiently trained or monitored in the proper use of equipment. Apropos of equipment failures it is of interest to note that the Food and Drug Administration issues a periodic bulletin (available to the public) which lists problems encountered with various medical devices, such as heart valve replacements, cardiac pacemakers, medication pumps.

Secondly are the hospital management failures or problems which can reflect themselves into the care of the hospitalized patient in a variety of ways, such as in the illustrations to follow. The budgetary consideration regarding personnel employment which may leave insufficient personnel to safely cover the ill and critically ill hospitalized patient. The poor personnel practices of a hospital which may lead to angry, disgruntled, poorly motivated personnel. The increased "patient load" on the insufficient number of personnel which produces an over extended and over scheduled staff and increases the likelihood of fatigue and inattention in the staff providing care to hospitalized patients. The insufficient time which is allocated by the hospital

Meyer Sonis M.D.

for the continuing education and staff development and in service training of personnel so that personnel may not be adequately prepared to perform and monitor "high tech" procedures. The pressure to perform high income producing procedures (i.e. x-rays, laboratory tests, diagnostic tests, surgery) which in turn places a burden on the performers (radiologists, pathologists, surgeons) to produce a high volume of these procedures while attempting to provide good care without haste. The lack of adequate attention by a hospital to maintaining an effective monitoring "safety net" for assuring sound, safe and quality care to hospitalized patients.

Medical Malpractice

Medical malpractice usually denotes a medical error and/or hospital mistake due to negligence and which produces a medical injury to a patient, and for which injury the patient or patient's family can seek legal redress and damages from the alleged perpetrators of the error or mistake. A medical malpractice claim is based on contract law or "tort law," namely the right of a person, who has contracted with another person to purchase their services or a product, to sue that person for damages due to an alleged breach in the contract. In a medical malpractice claim the person suing (plaintiff) must prove that: there was a medical injury of the plaintiff; this medical injury was caused by negligence of the physician and/or hospital; the physician and/or hospital (defendant) failed to act in keeping with medical standards established. In 1968, medical malpractice was defined in Black's Legal Dictionary as, a "bad, wrong or injudicious professional treatment of a patient and, in respect to the particular disease or injury, resulting in an injury, unnecessary suffering, or death to a patient and proceeding from ignorance, carelessness, want of professional skill, disregard of established rules, principles, neglect or a malicious criminal intent."

Skeletons in the Medical Closet
A Personal Story and a Professional Report

Medical malpractice suits were known in England in the late 1700's and were complained about in similar fashion as in modern times. Though much has been written about medical malpractice suits suffice to say that there is a continuing controversy regarding the need for reform of malpractice "tort" law, the efficacy of jury trials, the bias which can exist in judgments rendered, the length of time for closure of a claim, the outrageous damage awards, but to mention a few of these complaints. For the purpose of this book, my comments will concentrate on the nature and extent of medical malpractice, rather than the legal aspects.

In my recounting of my personal story it was intended to serve as a personalized example of an experience with medical error, medical injury of a patient, alleged medical negligence and with the legal process surrounding a claim of medical malpractice.

At one time in the historical evolution of medical malpractice litigation for iatrogenic injuries to patients, various medical publications (1958-1970) cited the "suit prone" patient as someone physicians in practice should be alert to. These patients were stereotyped as neurotic, dependent, uncooperative, hostile, demanding, cranky, dishonest, greedy, pushy, belligerent, unable to follow medical advice, full of unreal expectations from physicians. By 1970-1975 medical publications, medical professional organizations, medical insurance companies were clamoring about the medical malpractice crisis in the United States. They cited their concerns about: the increasing number of medical malpractice claims which were being filed; the increasing premiums which insurance carriers were charging physicians; the extraordinary damage payments which were being paid to plaintiffs; the rise in defensive medical care with costly and unneeded procedures because of a physician's fear of a legal suit; the reflection of these expenditures in the increasing cost of health care.

Meyer Sonis M.D.

This clamor reached such proportions as to ultimately involve the federal government in addressing these issues, problems and controversy via studies, reports and in congressional actions. By 1997 the GAO (Government Accounting Office) had issued thirteen reports on Medical Malpractice. These reports of studies were exclusively based on: reviews of studies conducted by others; survey questionnaires of insurance companies, depending on the self report of the insurance company; visits and interviews with selected officials of hospitals. Several of these reports will be briefly abstracted.

In 1986 the GAO (Government Accounting Office), at the request of the federal government, undertook a survey and report of thirty-seven nationally based organizations representing the legal, insurance and consumer interests on medical malpractice issues. Their principle findings were "that medical malpractice was a complicated problem with no easy answers; that no agreement could be reached among the interest groups surveyed regarding the problems, their severity, their solutions, or the proper role of states or the federal government."

In 1987, the GAO reported on a study of twenty-five insurance companies, randomly selected to represent one hundred and two companies in the United which collected 2.3 billion dollars in premiums in 1983 and which closed 74,000 claims for medical malpractice. Based on a pre-tested survey questionnaire completed by the insurance company, the GAO was able to compile data regarding medical malpractice events and resulting claims. Of all claims made almost 60% were closed with no payment, while 40% of all claims received a total of 2.6 billion dollars. Of all damages awarded, half of the claimants received $2,400 or less and the other half more than $2,400. Only 9% of claimants received $250,000 or more or 61% of all payments. Of all of the expenses incurred by insurance companies to dispose of a claim, 83% of these expenses were incurred by legal fees of the defense attorneys. Seventy-five percent of all claims closed involved allegations of surgical, diagnostic, treatment or obstetric errors and negligence. Regarding the severity of injury suffered by a patient due to medical error and negligence as alleged in the claim, 30% were of a temporary and minor consequence, 50% resulted in death, 4% in permanent total disability. Eighty percent of the claims closed involved an injury to a patient while hospitalized, while 13% occurred in a physician's office. Generally the more serious and severe injuries claimed by the patient took longer to resolve and close out than less serious claims. Of major interest was the fact that 42% of the physicians named in the claim as negligent had had a previous claim made against them. This number could be higher since no information was available in 28% of the cases. This latter report suggests that a medical malpractice claim may not necessarily serve as a deterrent.

By 1997 the GAO had conducted additional studies and surveys of the medical malpractice problems. In 1995, they reported results of a study of claims between 1989-1993 which indicated that 75% of claims were almost equally divided between surgery, failure to diagnose and improper treatment (similar to 1984 study); in 1995, they reported that 1% of national health care expenditures represent only a portion of all hospital and physician medical liability costs (medical insurance) while the other costs are passed on to the consumer. In 1986 the GAO reported on studies of medical malpractice in six states, which revealed "claims and insurance costs still rising despite reforms." In 1990, the GAO reported that: medical malpractice is a "continuing problem with far reaching implications;" "negligent medical malpractice must be addressed (citing data of the Harvard Studies);" "the compensation system for victims of malpractice needs refinement;" "the complexities involved in efforts to enhance overall quality of health care must be dealt with." In a later chapter, entitled Doctor & Hospital Watchdogs, I will focus on actions which have been taken to address the conclusions reached by the GAO.

Meyer Sonis M.D.

In line with the need in our country for more reliable data and information regarding medical malpractice, more scientifically based studies and their reports emerged between 1990 and 1997. These were studies which ranged from public reports of the Physician Insurers Association of America, to the malpractice claims data available as a quality improvement tool, to the problems of defensive medicine, to confronting the myths about jury incompetence, to outrageous awards in medical malpractice. I will cite only two examples of such studies and reports.

One such example is that of a series of studies which were strictly directed to the medical factors of each malpractice case and not the issues of law. This analysis of over 700 malpractice claims reported important areas of general surgery which were vulnerable to litigation as a result of: errors due to improper technical performance of surgery (37%), such as in bile duct injury during gall bladder surgery, nerve injury during thyroidectomy, major cranial nerve injury during head and neck surgery, delayed diagnosis of breast and rectal cancer. The study also reported that only 2% of medical injuries result in civil litigation.

The other example I will cite is from the Harvard Group studies (referred to earlier in this chapter) regarding adverse events to hospitalized patients. In their study and report (1991) on the relation between malpractice claims and adverse events due to negligence, they addressed two major questions about malpractice litigation: "how well it compensates patients who are actually harmed by medical negligence and whether it promotes quality and penalized substandard care." The method and results of this study, as with other studies of the Harvard Group, have become "gold standards" for medical malpractice investigations. In this study the Harvard Group matched the medical records of their random sample of hospitalized patients in New York in 1984 (which they reviewed) with statewide data on medical malpractice claims for that year. From this study they found that, despite the hue and cry about a malpractice claim crisis, only "2% of hospitalized patients who have had an adverse event judged negligent file a malpractice claim and that medical malpractice litigation infrequently compensates patients injured by medical negligence and rarely identifies and holds providers accountable for substandard practices."

What Can Be Done

Perhaps the greatest strides which have been made in our attempt to identify, prevent and correct medical injuries to hospitalized patients are to be found in three major developments of comparatively recent origin.

The first of these developments was the scientific rigor through which it was possible to collect reliable informative data about medical injuries caused by medical errors, medical negligence, hospital mistakes. The second of these developments was the enlightened approach of the body politic of organized medicine to bring the skeletons out of the medical closet and in placing medical errors within the framework of human errors. The third of these developments was that of the increased interest and concern of the lay public in becoming an informed patient.

On the matter of the first development I have addressed it through my personal story of what can happen and my professional report on baseline data pertinent to what can happen. On the matter of the second development I have addressed it in this chapter and will do so further in the chapter to follow. Finally on the matter of the third development I will address it through the several chapters of this book devoted to answering the questions of what the lay public should know about the medical industry, the hospital industry and the "doctor and hospital" watchers?

CHAPTER THREE

LESSONS TO BE LEARNED

About Medical Errors as System Failures

Medical errors have been known to be occurring, at least, since the days of antiquity. The approach to the prevention of this occurrence has also been known since the days of antiquity, namely find, blame and punish the perpetrator. Experience, since the days of antiquity, has shown us that this approach has not been a very fruitful one, in light of: the continued occurrence of medical errors; "repeat" perpetrators who did not seem to learn from their mistake; a "conspiracy of silence" which has surrounded the events of medical errors, hospital mistakes, medical malpractice.

This is not to say that physicians and hospitals were ignorant of or lackadaisical about the occurrence of medical errors and hospital mistakes. On the contrary the utilization by physicians and hospitals of various steps aimed at monitoring the occurrence of medical errors suggests the opposite. I am referring, for examples, to the mortality and morbidity conferences held by physicians and their hospitals in order to peer review the records of hospitalized patients who have suffered a poor outcome, or to the emphasis given traditionally by physicians and their hospitals to the need for autopsies and pathology reports as a way to learn from their mistakes. Rather this is to say that unfortunately the traditional approach of find, blame and punish the perpetrator tended to focus exclusively on the individual and the individual incident and was insufficiently focused on system failure as also a cause of such errors and mistakes. As stated by Dr. Leape (a major player in the Harvard Group Studies & Reports, 1994,) "the most important reason physicians and nurses have not developed more effective methods of error prevention or identification is that they have a great deal of difficulty in dealing with human error when it occurs, the reasons are to be found in the culture of medical practice which strives for error free practice." As also noted by Dr. Leape "students of human errors and performance reject this formulation, since both systems and individuals contribute to the problem."

With the emergence of a more enlightened approach to our understanding of medical errors and hospital mistakes beyond that of blame, as pioneered by the field of anesthesia some 30 years ago and as especially suggested in the first national conference on medical errors, perhaps we have opened the door to a more fruitful way to deal with medical errors and hospital mistakes. The gist of this enlightened approach was nicely stated in the magazine section of the New York Times of June 15, 1997 in the opening statement of their report on the national conference: "When fatal medical blunders occur the terse first question has usually been 'Who did it?' Now and then, with the help of a discipline called human factor analysts, hospitals are learning to ask instead, 'How can we save the next victim?'"

As our modern industrial society began to increasingly rely on high technology and technological experts to invent, develop and operate the machines, tools, equipment required by our industries, so has our awareness been heightened about the need for more information regarding the interface between the human and machine in the operation of our industries. Despite the variety of differences between industries, they all have at least two factors in common, namely: they all involve technology, tools, machines, and equipment; they all involve an interface between the human operator and the machine. Usually, or perhaps most of the time, the human "employee" who performs the tasks which interface with the machine does so successfully, but sometimes not so. Some of these errors can be minor, but some can be serious, tragic or costly.

Meyer Sonis M.D.

It has been rather difficult to come by reliable data on the extent to which human errors do occur in industry, and possibly for similar reasons as with medical errors. However, there have been various studies reported on in the published literature as well as by several speakers at the National Conference On Medical Errors. From such reports it is estimated that across all industrial systems the average incidence of failures due to human error was 60% (ranging from 90% in the airline industry, to 19% in the oil industry) as compared to 40% due to mechanical/equipment failure. Most of the knowledge which has been generated about the human-machine interface and human errors has come from the scientific and empiric studies of disciplines such as human factor analysts, cognitive psychologists and safety engineers. It is this knowledge which has been applied in seeking out the causes of various infamous system failures such as at Three Mile Island, Chernobyl, T.W.A.800 crash, the Challenger tragedy, the major oil spills and railroad crashes. It is the knowledge from these disciplines which has been utilized to design methods, procedures, equipment by which to minimize and prevent human errors in the human-machine interface. It is knowledge which has been based on the assumption that human errors are inevitable in the human-machine interface and that it is possible to anticipate, prevent and override such "human errors." It has been suggested that this knowledge, about human errors in the human-machine interface, can also be applicable in our understanding and correction of medical errors and hospital mistakes.

Given the fact that a hospital is a setting in which a complex mix of employees, machines, equipment, procedures, programs, patients interface and interact with each other, it should not take a great deal of imagination to see similarities between a hospital and other human-machine operations. The examples to follow can illustrate this point. The hospital provides different settings (the operating room, the emergency room, the x-ray room, the clinical laboratories, the intensive care unit) for rendering of medical and hospital care, with each of these settings operating or functioning independent of each other and with different purposes and equipment, procedures and staff. At the same time, the hospital employs a wide range of employees of differing professions, disciplines, technical skills, each with different educational requirements, different functions and responsibilities. At the same time, the hospital renders its programs through its differing employees to different patients, each with individual medical and surgical problems, varying diagnoses and treatment regimes, differing food habits, and in differing stages of illness or recovery. At the same time the hospital utilizes a variety of technological machines, equipment and instruments which must be operated by employees who are knowledgeable about the operation and maintenance of these machines. To give a sense of this complex mix, a recent study of a hospital intensive care unit reported that 178 different activities were performed on each patient daily. It should not be surprising, therefore, to learn that the more procedures and activities which are performed on a patient by "differing human hands" the greater are the risks for the occurrence of a human error.

As a consequence of the contributions of the various disciplines referred to, information and data has been generated which sheds light on our understanding of system management failure or the occurrence of human errors within the complex mix setting of humans and technology (machine), such as in industry or in the hospital. Further information and data has been generated which sheds light on our understanding of how and why human errors can occur. For the purposes of this book I will not report the details of this information and data, but rather I will refer the reader to the selected bibliography in the Appendix. Instead, I will abstract and extrapolate this information for the lay reader.

From studies of the successful and unsuccessful performance of the human operator across various complex work settings it has been possible to demonstrate the vital role played by the management/administration/managers/executives of an organizational system (industry, company, hospital) in influencing the behavior of the personnel who perform the tasks needed for the system to operate. It is the management/managers/executives of the system who make the basic decisions regarding the policy and directions, the infrastructure, the design and purchase of equipment, personnel required for the industry or hospital system, but to mention a few of the work setting factors which influence the performance behavior of system operators. I am referring, for examples, to work setting factors which can influence the manner of human performance through poor noise abatement, inadequate lighting, lack of safety measures, employment practices, poor equipment, discouragement of complaints, inadequate training of personnel, insufficient personnel. It is within such a work setting that persons who perform the tasks of system operation tend to be only one link in a long chain of accumulated problems in the system which can lead to potential accidents waiting to happen. Further, it is of interest to note that these studies also revealed that there were some work settings which supported and stimulated employees to pass information to system managers regarding potential problems so that system management can take steps of prevention or correction.

About Medical Errors as Human Failures

In the previous section of this chapter I reported, albeit briefly, information regarding the influence of failures in the work setting system on the occurrence of medical errors. In this section I will report, also briefly, information regarding the influence of human failures on the occurrence of medical errors. This latter information suggests a basis by which: to understand how human failures do, can, and will continue to occur, namely, the way in which the human organism is built and wired; to understand the reason(s) or the why human failures do, can and will continue to occur, namely, the way in which aberrations or

Skeletons in the Medical Closet
A Personal Story and a Professional Report

interruptions interfere with the normal process of the wiring of the human organism to acquire, utilize, retrieve information (the process of mental and cognitive function).

Through the template of a genetic blueprint the trajectory of biological evolution of living organisms, from the earlier model of the one celled organism to the latest model of the human organism, has led to a structure in the organism which is capable of supporting the function of that organism. In the human organism, as the latest model of biological evolution, the human organism has many features of its structure in common with earlier models but also features which have been accommodated to support the functions of the human organism which are different than other organisms.

Thus the human organism has had built into it, for examples: a <u>framework of bones,</u> which are capable of motion so that the human can stand, walk erect, crawl, sit, squat, run, climb; <u>a set of teeth</u> which allows the human to eat and chew the kind of food needed; <u>a collection of cells</u> which are capable of ultimately becoming the various organs of the human body each with different purposes such as digestion of the kind of food the human eats, elimination, absorption, pumping circulation, vocalization, breathing, seeing, hearing, tasting, touching, smelling; <u>a network of cells and muscles</u> which are structured in such a way as to form the tubes and canals needed to circulate and distribute the nutrients and chemicals required by the various organs and to collect and eliminate the waste material produced by the organs.

Thus the human organism has had built into it for examples: <u>a variety of cells and secretory organs,</u> which are capable of serving as timing and sequence "clocks" for initiating, stopping, monitoring and governing the orderly sequence of cell growth and development; <u>other cells and organs</u> which govern the rhythmic and periodic production and secretion of the hormones and enzymes required for growth and development, in keeping with a pattern of circadian rhythm (night and day).

Meyer Sonis M.D.

Thus the human organism has had built into it for examples: <u>a collection of cells</u> which are capable of producing or generating an electrical charge due to the ionic (electronic) differences between the chemicals inside and outside of the cell; <u>a network of these cells</u> which are connected or contiguous to each other from the head to toe of the organism so that they form a highway or conductor pathway for transmission of "electrical" signals from one cell to the other; the <u>coalescence of these different "neuronic"</u> cells into the nervous system organs of a brain, spinal chord and nerves, which serve as a receiver and transmitter of signals to all other organs/glands.

Finally, but perhaps of greater relevance to our understanding of human failures, the results of the genetic trajectory of biologic evolution of living organisms led to structures and functions which supported the ability of the organism to learn (or be trained) so that the organism could respond and adapt appropriately to its internal and external environment. This ability to learn has been demonstrated and documented, for a few examples, by the studies of Kanel on the lowly earthworm to Pavlov's dogs to Skinner's mice to Washoe's sign language response. In addition to the building in and wiring of an organism's ability to learn and remember, the genetic trajectory of biologic evolution of living organisms took one more step of evolution in its latest model, namely that of an expanded brain size, mass and structure of the human organism in order to accommodate the human functions of mental and cognitive processing. Thus the human organism has been set up to receive, act on and transmit information from and to its internal organs, from and to its sense organs of seeing, smelling, hearing, tasting, touching, and from and to its external environment. It is this "neuronal" highway which enables the brain/its network of nerves to receive, encode and transmit information from within the body (internal information) regarding the continuing operation and homeo-stasis of organs systems and cells, as well as to receive, encode and transmit

Skeletons in the Medical Closet
A Personal Story and a Professional Report

information from outside the body (external information) regarding the surrounding environment (seeing, hearing, tasting, smelling, touching).

One form of action in response to internal information which the human can perform, but in common with other organism, is that which is required to maintain the vital functions of living, such as breathing, heart pumping, circulation of blood/fluids/nutrients to the organs, excretion of waste products due to metabolism, regulation of internal secretions. These are actions which are taken automatically and are not under the voluntary control of the human organism.

Another form of action which the human can perform in response to a danger or threat is that of "flight or fight" in order to protect the human for survival. This action is shared in common with other organisms. It is an action which is almost automatic in that it is a reflex action, such as immediately removing a hand from a hot stove.

And then there is an action which only the human organism can perform because of the special structure and function of its brain, namely, the process of mental and cognitive functioning (to acquire/encode/store/retrieve information to learn, think, imagine, speak, remember, symbolize). It is from the contributions of cognitive psychologists that much of our current understanding has been generated about the normal process of mental and cognitive functioning and the actions resulting from this process.

As a consequence of cognitive studies, cognitive psychologists believe that the human brain is wired in such a way as to enable it to process and act on information (i.e. the process of mental and cognitive functioning) in any of several ways.

In their view most mental functioning (securing, retrieving and acting on information) is a process which is fast, automatic, effortless (requires little conscious effort) and routine. Because the brain can store a vast array of prepackaged information

Meyer Sonis M.D.

which has been acquired through repetitive learning/practice/experience, it is possible for this information to be retrieved and acted on rather quickly and routinely and without much conscious thought. Examples of such routine actions are: the steps taken by me when I shave; the actions taken by me in driving from my home to my office; the steps taken by a surgeon in performing his 50th appendectomy. In other words the more expert a human is at "something," the larger the number of prepackaged programmed instructions in his/her brain, and the faster the pace for performing an action.

In their view, some mental functioning in the human is processed at a slower pace, in a much less routine manner and with greater conscious effort. This kind of mental functioning is called "rule based," since it follows a rule that if X happens in the performance of a routine action then follow by action Y. An example of such a mental functioning process is as follows: if a surgeon who performs a routine appendectomy does not find the appendix in its usual location (X), then the surgeon knows (Y) to search and see if the appendix has curled up on itself, which it sometimes does. And finally some mental functioning is processed even slower and requires much more conscious effort to carry out because it is based on acquisition of a very technical knowledge required for the performance of a specific action. This last kind of process comes into play for example, when the neuro-surgeon is conducting a micro-dissection requiring thinking through of every step before proceeding to the next step.

In the view of these experts they believe that regardless of the type of mental functioning process the occurrence of a human failure is caused by an interruption or aberration in the normal process of mental functioning. Such an interruption in the process can be produced by: damage or defect in the cognitive apparatus, namely, the brain, (as in Alzheimer disease, brain trauma, congenital defects); physiologic factors, as in boredom, loss of sleep, overwork, fatigue, illness, drug and alcohol abuse;

Skeletons in the Medical Closet
A Personal Story and a Professional Report

psychological factors, as in boredom, preoccupation, inattention, poor motivation and the various human frailties; environmental factors, as in a toxic atmosphere; system management problems as in noise, inadequate light, over scheduling, poor working conditions, insufficient training of personnel, equipment failure.

By The Physician

The lessons which should be learned by a physician about the potential of his/her making of a medical error and the impact of this on a patient and the patient's family should begin on his/her entrance to medical school. These lessons should begin at the time of physician's initial encounter with his/her patient and continue on through the patient's career with him/her, prior to, during and after hospitalization.

The lessons which the physician should be learning are lifetime lessons in the practice of the art and science of medicine. They are continuous lessons in upgrading his/her knowledge and skill, recognizing his/her capabilities and limits and need for help if required, accepting his/her fallibility and need for monitoring.

These are the lessons which the physician should be learning about the potential of an adverse event occurring to his/her patient and about the human relationship aspect of the practice of medicine, which so often is neglected by the medical profession.

Too often the informed consent of the patient and patient's family to hospitalization and its procedures becomes a perfunctory or meaningless consent rather than a consent of an informed patient and family. Short of an emergency, patients should be given this information prior to their hospitalization. In providing this information to the patient and/or family, the physician should encourage questions from the patient, answer all questions posed, assure himself/herself that the information is understood by the patient. Such information should at least answer the following questions. Why and for what reason(s) is the patient to be hospitalized? What kind of hospital is it? Is it a teaching hospital in which medical students, interns and residents will be involved in the direct care of the patient? Does the hospital meet the standards established by the appropriate accreditation and licensing bodies? Is there a physician or physicians on the premises at all times? Who, of the physicians caring for the patient during hospitalization, will be responsible for decisions and communication with the patient and/or his/her family on all matters of pertinence to the medical/surgical care of the patient? If procedures are to be performed, what are the reasons for such? What will be done? Who will be performing the procedure(s)? What experience does the person performing the procedure have in the conduct of this procedure? What are the risks and benefits of this procedure? What is the anticipated outcome of performing the procedure or of not performing the procedure? How long might the patient remain in the hospital? What services and procedures are covered by the insurance carrier of the patient?

During the course of hospitalization, all physicians (i.e., house staff, consultants, anesthesiologist, surgeon, etc.) who will have direct contact with the patient should provide the patient with information about themselves (i.e., their title, specialty, experience, etc.), the purpose of their contact, the procedures to be performed (i.e., details, risks, benefits, complications, etc.), medications recommended (i.e., purpose, adverse reactions, side effects, etc.)

In the event of an unanticipated adverse event, regardless of whether this was a minor/inconsequential event or a major/life threatening event, the physician responsible for the care of the patient should forthrightly inform the patient and/or family about the event. The physician should explain. What happened? Why did it happen? What are the consequences? What can be done to correct the complications of the adverse event? What is the ultimate outcome? The responsible physician should encourage questions from the patient and/or family and should answer these questions as completely as possible. If the adverse event leads to a poor prognosis or death of the patient, the physician responsible for the total care of that patient must be available to help the patient and/or family with their anger, their guilt, their questions/concerns/ anxiety, and their grief.

By The Medical Educator

For those physicians who assume responsibility as medical educators for the education and training of medical students, resident house staff and practicing physicians, they must become more alert and attentive to the newer knowledge about human disease/illness/injury, to the newer knowledge we have available about the human factors in medical injuries, to the occurrence of medical injuries, to the prevention of such and to the system in which health care takes place and in which medical injuries occur.

The medical educator must become more comfortable in dealing with the "skeletons" in the medical closet which have become intertwined with the conspiracy of silence. The medical educator must become a more effective "role model" for the novice physician in wanting to learn from mistakes and in wanting to feel free to report, discuss and seek help regarding medical errors which occur.

The medical educator must seek ways and means to change the traditional and ineffective approach to the continuing education of practicing physicians in order to more reliably influence practice acquisition by the physician of new skills/information, including that of a self critical attitude regarding the potential for errors and mistakes. The medical educator must take the "lead" in calling for health system changes which would include more adequate monitoring of the failures and mistakes of the system.

All medical students and house staff physicians (residents) must be taught about their potential role and responsibility in the occurrence of adverse events, the prevention of such occurrences, in remediation of the consequences of adverse events, and in helping the patient and patient's family to cope with the outcome of an adverse event. Unfortunately medical school curricula and medical school faculty do not pay sufficient attention to discussions or presentations of the various factors which are of relevance to the causes and consequences of adverse events occurring to hospitalized patients. I am referring to, for examples, factors such as the heavy schedule of duties and responsibilities carried by a house staff physician, the frequency of evening coverage, the inadequacy of supervision, and all of which may produce an overburdened physician who is less alert and less informed about his/her patients. I am also referring, for example, to the double bind situation in which house staff physicians are often placed, namely, they are, on the one hand viewed as problem residents by their superiors if they call for "help" too often or if, on the other hand, they do not call for "help" in the event of a deteriorating patient, so that it becomes difficult for residents to acknowledge their limits of knowledge, skill and fallibility.

By The Hospital

At present, there are approximately 6,000 community hospitals in the United States, into which an estimated 30+ million patients will be admitted during the course of a year. As the data previously referred to suggests it can be expected that for most of these patients, their hospitalization will be a successful and satisfactory experience. It can also be expected that 4% of these patients will suffer a medical injury due to medical errors or hospital mistakes. A review of this data should make it abundantly clear to hospitals, their governing bodies, their executive staff, that they must take the leadership in learning the lessons about system changes which are supportive of preventing medical injuries, identifying and reporting such

Skeletons in the Medical Closet
A Personal Story and a Professional Report

injuries, helping the patient and his/her family cope with the results of medical injuries.

Teaching hospitals must bear a good deal of responsibility for effecting system changes in hospital care because of the greater frequency of medical injuries in teaching hospitals than in other hospitals. It is in the teaching hospitals that more seriously ill patients are found than in non-teaching hospitals and which increases the frequency of complications, more invasive procedures, higher risk patients for medical injuries.

Hospitals, whether teaching or non-teaching hospitals, must assume the leadership role for: more careful perusal of a physician's credentials to conduct his/her practice; monitoring a physician's performance; identifying, preventing and helping the impaired physician; supporting changes in the attitude and behavior of the medical staff from a blame and shame approach for medical errors to the newer approach for a more effective means of reporting and preventing medical errors and hospital mistakes.

I am referring for examples to system changes in a hospital which only the administration and medical leadership of the hospital can allow to happen, such as: monitoring unnecessary admissions, procedures, studies, surgery; minimizing an environment of stress and strain on personnel from insufficient number of staff, overworked staff; minimizing the performance of procedures for which the staff is not trained; supporting safety measures for patient care by diligence on equipment maintenance, machine replacement.

There is a final lesson which should be learned by hospitals about their adverse events, but which hospitals seem to have difficulty learning. I am referring to the fact that when an adverse event occurs in a hospital, all parties to the adverse event are hurting, including both the patient and his/her family as well as the hospital and its staff. When such an adverse event occurs, the hospital and its physicians, and not simply the hospital attorney and risk management personnel, must devote more of their energy and attention to participation with the patient and/or his or her family in seeking mutual answers to questions of what happened, why, what needs to be done, rather than immediately assuming and placing the patient and the patient's family in an adversarial role.

Too often, the hospital and physician forget that the management of risk concerns a patient, and not just the risk of the hospital and physician. Just as there is the lesson for the medical profession in needing to help the patient and his/her family cope with the consequences of an adverse event, there is the lesson for the hospital in utilizing its resources, tools, information to inform and help the patient and his/her family cope with the consequences of the adverse event. It is to be noted by hospitals, which are so fearful of being sued, that despite the hue and cry about malpractice suits, recent studies have documented how few patients or their families do take legal action regarding their experiences with adverse events.

By Accreditation And Licensing Authorities

Scientific studies have now supported the view that practice does make "perfect" in the performance of highly technical and "risky" medical/surgical procedures. For this reason, a trend is emerging in our country to concentrate the performance of such "risky" procedures in "Centers of Excellence" (hospitals which perform a larger volume of invasive procedures, surgery, high tech studies). Thus, it is entirely possible that within such a high volume/high income/high repute hospital: there may be inadequate supervision of house staff in their care of post-surgical critically ill patients by the attending staff; the surgical house staff may be over scheduled and overburdened; there may be insufficient opportunity and productive energy for the surgical house staff to learn, study and devote the required time for learning to perform highly technical procedures while also attempting to render ordinary patient care, let alone intensive patient care to the critically ill patient; there may be difficulty for the busy surgical "teachers" to identify and help the house staff who may be having difficulty with their skill, clinical judgment and their ability to seek timely "help."

It therefore behooves accreditation authorities to develop criteria, for approval of a hospital, which can pay equal attention to the "quality" of house staff training in a high volume "Center of Excellence" and to the "quantity" of procedures performed by this house staff. It behooves the third party payors (in their peer review of a hospital) to develop more effective mechanisms, than currently are in use by them, for monitoring/assessing the quality and safety of care rendered to patients within such "Centers of Excellence," and to disclose their findings to the public. It behooves these authorities to become much more diligent and responsible in their continuous monitoring of those hospitals with "poor" track records and those physicians with "poor" track records.

By The Hospitalized Patient

It is indeed fortunate that the average lay person now has access to more information about hospitals, their physicians and staff, hospital practices, and the success or lack of success of a hospital in providing quality and safety in their medical and surgical care. I am referring to the various public report cards on hospitals, doctors and medical care and which can be secured from a variety of sources, such as listed in the appendix. This information, as recently as ten years ago, would have been difficult to secure. And yet, despite this progress on behalf of the public good, the average lay person has done very little to avail themselves of this information nor have the medical and hospital industries done much to help the patient know about this information.

The average lay person can become an informed patient. It is an informed patient who is capable of becoming an active partner, and not simply a passive receptacle, in his/her medical care while hospitalized. They can serve as a partner with the hospital and doctors in the clinical services rendered. The informed patient can provide medical and health information about themselves and raise pertinent questions. The informed patient can change their own negative health behavior. With "Let the Buyer Beware" in mind, the hospitalized person can be fore-armed with information and thus forewarned.

The informed patient should know about their own medical history, their family medical history, past medical studies which may have been performed (i.e., what, why, when, where, by whom, results), past hospitalization (reasons, where, when, what was done, outcome). Further, they should know about their current medications, past medications, and their own health behavior (smoking, safe sex, exercise, etc.). Before an admission to a hospital, as well as during hospitalization, the informed patient must learn to not be shy or wary of asking questions and seeking clarification from all persons who are providing them with medical, surgical, nursing care. Informed patients have the right to know about the hospital and its ability to take care of them, the personnel serving them, the reasons for their hospitalization, the procedure to be performed, the experience of hospital staff in the procedures to be performed, the medications prescribed. In summary the informed patient has the obligation to themselves to seek and secure the information required by them.

Final Lesson For Physicians, Hospitals And Accreditation Bodies

In searching for a way to conclude this chapter, I could think of no better way to do this than by an extensive quote from the JAMA News story (Oct. 27, 1997), which was written by their own correspondent.

Skeletons in the Medical Closet
A Personal Story and a Professional Report

"Once upon a stupid time, it was possible to start a car in reverse. Many people backed into their garages, and a few ran over their children. The automobile industry redesigned automatic transmissions, and now you cannot start a car in reverse. End of problem. End of these accidental deaths. The health care industry is about to be redesigned. Granted, it won't be as quick or as simple to do, but the new National Patient Safety Foundation at the AMA has begun working to create a smarter, safer health care environment to help prevent accidental injuries and deaths.

Imagine working in an environment in which:

- All physicians routinely practice crisis management skills in realistic simulations, using computerized dummies for patients.
- All hospitals use electronic medical records, eliminating errors related to a doctor's illegible handwriting. All prescription orders, including those from a doctor's office, are entered into a computer that remembers that the patient is allergic to certain drugs even if the doctor forgets. It also can immediately spit out facts such as what other drugs the patient is taking that interact with the new prescription. The same kind of bar code technology found in supermarkets is used religiously to track medications given to patients in hospitals. Hospitals don't permit double shifts or impossible work schedules for interns and residents.
- Concentrated potassium chloride, the cause of five to 10 hospital deaths every year, comes off the shelves in hospital units.
- Doctors and nurses work in teams so they can understand how to support and help one another.
- Medications cannot have similar labels.

Meyer Sonis M.D.

- Equipment is designed so that it is impossible to place a solution into the intravenous tube which was designed to go into a gastrostomy tube."

CHAPTER FOUR

THE PHYSICIAN INDUSTRY

Introduction

In this and the next chapter, I will be reporting on The Physician and Hospital Industries which are two components of the medical industrial complex in the United States. Among other components of this medical industrial complex, but to mention a few, are the Pharmaceutical Industry (producers of medications and related substances), the Medical & Surgical Supplies Industry (makers of various supplies utilized by physicians and hospitals for patient diagnosis and treatment), the Medical & Surgical Equipment Industry (makers of x-rays, nuclear magnetic radiation, x-ray film, surgical instruments, stethoscopes), the Clinical Laboratories Industry (utilized by physicians and others to conduct patient clinical studies), the Radioactive Waste Industry (collection and disposal of radioactive chemicals and material utilized in patient care).

My reason for focusing on only these two components is because they are more relevant to the theme of this book, namely, injuries, medical errors, hospital mistakes and medical malpractice.

Ordinarily when reference is made to the term of an industrial complex, such as the military industrial complex, the investment and financial complex, the fuel industrial complex or others, these industries are viewed as synonymous with a profit making industry. In the situation of the medical industrial complex, however, it is a mix of private not for-profit corporations, public not-for-profit corporations and private for-profit corporations.

For purposes of this chapter I have designated physicians, who earn an income and pay taxes on that income, as members of The Physician Industry because this income collectively is big business. For illustration of this point, data sources available (Medical Economics, Government Accounting Office) estimate that the gross income for active individual physicians (not retired) ranges from $68,000 to $400,000 annually. In 1991 there were 800,000 physicians in the United States of which 600,000 were in active clinical practice. Taken altogether and at the lowest income range for physicians, 40 billion dollars in annual income was generated. By anybody's standards this is Big Business.

In this country in order to be viewed as an active physician certain minimum requirements must be met. He or she as a physician: must have successfully completed a four year course of medical education to earn a Medical Doctor (M.D.) or Osteopathic Doctor (D.O.) degree from a school of medicine, which has been approved by the appropriate national accreditation authorities; and must have successfully completed a minimum of a one year internship in a hospital which has been approved by the appropriate national accreditation authorities; and must have successfully passed an examination for medical licensure which is given and granted by the appropriate State Board of Medical Licensure in the given state in which the physician will practice. In meeting this minimum requirement the physician will now be enabled by law to provide clinical care (diagnose, treat, prescribe medications) under his or her own authority and responsibility without the supervision of others. Further this license of a physician to practice medicine is usually a lifetime license unless revoked.

Physician Facts And Characteristics

From the point of view of this chapter namely to provide information on the extent to which this Physician Industry through its members are directly and or indirectly involved in perpetrating medical errors and malpractice, the information has generally not been available or accessible to the public, because of the continued conspiracy of silence and confidentiality which has surrounded these occurrences. It is only more recently, and primarily under the pressure of others outside of The Physician Industry, that such information is seeing the light of day. I have referred to such information in a previous chapter. Though most physicians are not involved in the events of medical errors and malpractice, some of these physicians however are. For this reason the public should have some knowledge about physicians in general.

The majority of physicians have earned their M.D. degree from an Allopathic School of Medicine, while the rest have earned their M.D. degree from a Foreign Medical School or earned their D.O. degree from an Osteopathic School of Medicine. Though there are distinctions between the M.D. and D.O. degree and which will be detailed elsewhere in this chapter, this distinction has almost become nonexistent currently.

From data available (Physician Trends and Characteristics of the American Medical Association) there currently are 600,000 to 650,000 physicians in the United States who are active, not retired or federal employees. Some of these physicians can be categorized as a primary care physician, namely a physician from whom a patient can receive routine, sustained and continued medical care for all of their medical complaints, as well as referral to a secondary care physician (specialist) if needed. A secondary care physician is one from whom a patient can receive sporadic and periodic medical care for the diagnosis and treatment of more complex and serious medical and surgical disorders. The majority of primary care physicians are those who practice as general practitioners, family practitioners or pediatricians (with the latter two having specialized training, described elsewhere in this chapter). Occasionally a primary care physician will be trained as a specialist in internal medicine. In most cases the secondary care physician is a physician who has been trained in any one or several medical or surgical specialties or who has self-designated himself/herself as a specialist (again, details of which will be provided in a later section of this chapter).

In the best of all medical care worlds, it is the well trained primary care physicians who can best serve the long term interests of a patient through continuous, comprehensive and coordinated care. It is this physician who can provide holistic care, paying attention to the psycho-social-biological needs of the patient, and who can monitor and guard against fragmentation of the patient's medical and surgical care. It is this physician who can come closest to the image of the old fashioned doctor who knew the family, came on house calls, could recall the various past medical problems of the patient and could judiciously orchestrate the patient through the maze of tests, specialists, and diseases. In practice, however, this ideal is only sometimes reached. It is only during the past two decades, and under the pressure for keeping medical costs down, that consideration for changes in health care delivery are converging towards this ideal, namely placing the primary care physician in a position to serve as the gatekeeper to all medical and surgical care and to the utilization of laboratory tests, studies, procedures, specialists, hospitalization by a patient.

Some primary care physicians still conduct their practice within their own homes in a residential community, as was so often done in the past by general practitioners, so that their office is easily accessible to patients residing in that area. Some physicians, as is so often done by specialists, may conduct their practice within a commercial building, a hospital or medical building complex, so that their patients require consideration of transportation and parking. For some physicians their offices and furnishings are rather simple, while for other physicians their offices and furnishings are quite elegant, spacious and comfortable.

Under the current pressures of medical cost containment, medical competition, managed care, population capitation ("pooling" of costs of patient care), significant changes in the organization and structure of medical practice have emerged and probably will continue to do so at an increased pace. Though some physicians still conduct their practice in the organizational structure of a "solo" practitioner, that is, a physician who is self employed and practices entirely on his or her own in generating his or her income on a for-profit basis, this style is on the decrease. On the increase are the number of physicians who conduct their practice in one of several types of "group" practice: several doctors, each of the same specialty or primary care category, who each see their own patients but who share expenses of office and staff and who cover for each other during nights, weekends or holidays or vacations; several doctors, each of different specialties who share office space, expenses, staff and who each see their own patients but refer patients to the other doctors in the group. On the increase are the number of physicians: who are of different specialties (including primary care) but who collectively band together as "legal partners" and/or "for-profit corporations," so as to act like a coalition of physicians able to "bargain" with a third party payor for a contract to deliver health care to a designated population and/or geographic area; who have become salaried employees of a not for-profit or a public health provider (i.e. Hospital, Geriatric Center, Medical School, Ambulatory Center, etc.); who have become salaried employees of a for-profit health care provider (i.e. Health Maintenance Organization, Managed Care, Corporate Medicine, etc.). Of more recent vintage there are physician groups who are purchased by a profit or non-profit hospital for a cash settlement and then employed by the hospital as salaried employees plus benefits and now has come unionization of physicians.

Some physicians (and primarily those in primary care solo practice) may have limited equipment and trained staff for this equipment (i.e. x-ray, clinical laboratory, physiotherapy) so that they may require referral of their patients elsewhere for these procedures. Other physicians, primarily those in specialty practice and/or group practices, may have a greater capability for providing a more comprehensive array of procedures and thus equipment and trained staff. With the former physician may come an under utilization of needed procedures while with the latter an over utilization of unneeded procedures.

Some physicians may be very communicative with their patients and feel very comfortable in: encouraging their patients to ask questions and in answering these questions; explaining the diagnosis and treatment of their patient's medical/surgical problems; providing the patient with information about the reasons for recommending studies, (including information about the procedures and studies as well as the risks and benefits related to the procedures and studies) and in sharing the results of these studies; sharing information with the patient from medical records of their patient, if requested to do so; providing their patients with copies of pertinent reports, etc.; discussing fees with their patients. Other physicians, who may be as equally competent as is the communicative physician, may not share the same empathetic attitude to their patients and their patients' concerns, questions and rights.

For some patients the decision to select a physician may be precipitated by the immediate need of a current medical complaint or discomfort so that the various considerations in seeking a primary care doctor become of secondary importance to the patient. For these patients the phrase "any port in a storm" may be their motto. For other patients, the decision to select a physician may be the result of an organized process of planning for the eventuality of needing medical attention, so that serious consideration is given to seeking information about a physician to serve as their primary care physician. For some patients the choice of a physician may be based on the advice of neighbors, friends, word of mouth, other family members, geographic proximity of the physician, fellow workers in the work place, or parents of other children. For some patients the choice of a physician may be based on information about the doctor from a variety of sources, such as the local medical society, hospital referral center, nurse or physician acquaintances, professional directories, public library, or social agencies. For some patients it may be of minor consequence to them if their physician is communicative and welcomes questions or if they themselves are informed consumers, while for other patients this may not be so.

All in all, and as can be surmised from the above comments, there are an infinite number of ways by which to describe the characteristics of a physician, their practices and practice styles, as there are ways to describe the personal preferences of patients in selecting a physician. Regardless of this diversity, however, there is a basic set of information about a physician which every patient should secure in order to become a more informed consumer of medical care and to increase their chances of securing safe, competent and quality medical care. There is now a growing body of literature for the lay person, which can be of help to them in answering the question of what should you know about your physician? For purposes of reference about such sources of information attention is called to the selected Bibliography (see Appendix).

Additional Factoids About The Physician Industry

Of the almost 800,000 active physicians in the United States approximately 80% are engaged in clinical practice (seeing patients) while 20% of them are engaged in medical education (medical students, interns and residents), conducting medical research, medical administration (operation of a Medical School, Hospital, Health Care Facility). By far most of these physicians (75% to 80%) are graduates of American Medical and Osteopathic Schools, while 20% to 25% are graduates of Foreign Medical Schools (FMG). The number of Foreign Medical Graduates who are now active physicians in the United States has doubled during the past twenty years as a consequence of a "shortage" of physicians in selected geographic areas (rural, urban minority populations), the unequal geographic distribution of physicians and the increased financial rewards of medical practice in the United States as compared with other countries. It is of interest to note that, generally speaking but with the exceptions of a few countries, graduates of foreign medical schools are not as adequately prepared for medical practice in keeping with the standards established as are graduates of American medical schools. For this reason FMG's are required to pass certain educational tests and/or secure additional training before being allowed to practice medicine in the United States.

As displayed in Table 1, the distribution of physicians varies from one geographic region to the other.

TABLE 1

GEOGRAPHIC DISTRIBUTION OF ALL PHYSICIANS

IN THE UNITED STATES

	BY REGION	BY PHYSICIAN TO POPULATION RATIO
NORTHEAST	26%	1 per 300 persons
SOUTH	30%	1 per 800 persons
MIDWEST	22%	1 per 500 persons
WEST	22%	1 per 600 persons

(SOURCE: 1990, AMA Demographic Profile)

Further, it should be noted that this unequal distribution of physicians is even more marked within the same region so that, for examples, the number of physicians per 100,000 persons ranges: in the Northeast from a high of 354 in New York State to a low of 174 in New Hampshire; in the South from a high of 396 in Georgia to a low of 138 in Mississippi; in the Midwest from a high of 246 in Illinois to a low of 149 in South Dakota; or in the West from a high of 274 in California to a low of 116 in Wyoming. Of the various states in the United States, the five states with the highest physician to population ratio are (in descending order) the District of Columbia, Maryland, Massachusetts, New York, and Connecticut, while the five lowest are (in descending order) Oklahoma, South Dakota, Wyoming, Alaska, and Idaho. In other words, while some geographic areas of our country may have an abundance of physicians available to serve their population, there are other areas which do not. For the past few decades these deficiencies in geographic distribution of physicians have persistently been found in rural areas, urban poverty areas, and minority population areas. It must also be kept in mind that the geographic availability of physicians to serve an area's population does not automatically assure the population of having access to the physicians, since that is much more a matter of economics and other factors.

It has been suggested that the reasons physicians locate themselves as they do, such as, mainly in urban or suburban rather than rural areas or urban poverty areas, is based on their personal lifestyles, the potential for increased income, the need to remain near academic medical centers, hospitals, and other professional resources. Some studies have suggested that if a physician has been born and reared in a rural setting, there is an increased possibility of his/her returning to a rural area to practice.

At the present time and continuing for the next decade or two, and as a consequence of the major changes and trends in health care delivery, it is postulated that this geographic regional distribution of physicians may undergo significant changes under the impetus of medical competition, physician economics of supply and demand, organizational changes in structures for delivery of medical care.

During the past two decades, and possibly continuing into the foreseeable future, there have been other changes in the characteristics of The Physician Industry, as reported in several articles. From 1965 to 1992 the number of physicians who served as primary care physicians increased by only 13%, whereas the number of physicians who served as specialists increased by 121%. The current supply of physicians (an average of 200 physicians/100,000 population) already exceeds the estimated number required to meet anticipated needs. Surveys suggest that physicians are not optimally prepared to meet the health care needs of projected managed care systems. Other changes which have been noted during the past two decades in the characteristics of The Physician Industry are: a shift in the age distribution of physicians to an older age population, with almost half of the physicians 45 years of age or older; a shift in the number of women physicians from 2% of the total to almost 15% of the total; a shift upwards in the number of Osteopathic Physicians; a shift upwards in full time salaried physicians, and with the majority of these physicians having less than two years experience. Apropos of these demographic shifts, it should be noted that most physicians who graduated medical schools 20 or more years ago have forgotten about half of the information acquired by them during medical school, let alone been able to keep up with the newer knowledge generated, even with continuing medical education.

By meeting the minimum requirements for a physician to practice medicine it has been assumed by law, regulation and tradition in our American society that each and every physician has acquired the basic knowledge, skill and ethics required to provide medical care which is safe, competent and of a quality in

Skeletons in the Medical Closet
A Personal Story and a Professional Report

keeping with standards established for such care. Further it has also been assumed that, regardless of the locale of medical education, internship and licensure examination of physicians, each physician will closely approximate each other in the basic knowledge, skill and ethics acquired because of the national standards established for medical education. It has now been shown that this assumption may not be totally valid.

Medical Education

In the past, three different types of medical schools existed, namely, an Allopathic Medical School leading to a Medical Doctor degree (M.D.), a Homeopathic Medical School leading to a Medical Doctor degree (M.D.), and an Osteopathic Medical School leading to an Osteopathic Doctor degree (D.O.). An Allopathic School of Medicine was based on a system of medical practice which utilizes all measures (whether empiric or scientifically proven of value) in the treatment of disease. A Homeopathic School of Medicine was based on a system of medical practice which treats a disease through administration of a minute dose of a medication that ordinarily would produce in a healthy person, the symptoms similar to the symptoms produced by the disease. An Osteopathic School of Medicine was based on a system of medical practice in which diseases were viewed as due chiefly to loss of structural (anatomical) integrity and therefore could be treated by "bony manipulation," as well as other methods. At the present point, and in practice, the distinctions between these different types of medical school are almost non-existent or blurred. Because of the preponderance in numbers of Allopathic Schools of Medicine as compared with the others, and in light of the blurring of distinctions between them, the remainder of my comments about medical schools and medical education will be exclusively focused on Allopathic Schools.

Meyer Sonis M.D.

At the present there are 125 schools of medicine providing medical education in the United States. These schools have been approved because they meet the standards established for medical education and granting of the M.D. degree by the appropriate accreditation authorities, namely the Council on Medical Education of the American Medical Association, and the American Association of Medical Colleges. These are the standards which are recognized by law, regulations, tradition, as governing medical education (called Undergraduate Medical Education) and thus have become the commonly agreed upon yardstick for: teaching all medical students the basic knowledge, skill and ethics required for medical practice; evaluation of the medical students on their acquisition of this required basic knowledge, skill and ethics.

Prior to 1900, there were no commonly agreed upon standards for medical education and medical schools so that the existing medical schools differed substantially in their curriculum, methods of teaching, criteria for admission of medical students. Many of these medical schools were private for profit apprenticeship enterprises. In fact, after standards were established in 1905, about one third of existing medical schools could not meet these minimum standards. Once standards were established they have been evaluated and modified periodically over the years to the present in order to reflect the progress made in medical knowledge and clinical care.

For the lay person it is sometimes difficult to comprehend the amount of information which must be acquired by a physician-to-be during a four year period of time, let alone to appreciate the newer and newer information which a physician must constantly learn. In my own medical lifetime of 55 years, knowledge for examples about organ transplantation, surgical repair of coronary arteries, nuclear magnetic resonance, genetic diseases, genetic modification, anti- biotics, antidepressants,

Skeletons in the Medical Closet
A Personal Story and a Professional Report

anti-psychotic medications were not known at the time I became a physician.

For the medical schools in the United States (and generally elsewhere) the information which must be taught to and acquired by a medical student over a four year period of time is similar from one school to another. Though there are differences in the format, timing and sequence utilized by one medical school from another in teaching the information required, the content of this information is basically categorized as information in the <u>basic sciences</u> (generally taught in the first two years as building blocks) and information in the <u>clinical sciences</u> (usually taught in the last two years of medical education).

In an oversimplified description the <u>basic sciences</u> consist of information about: the structure of the body and all of its constituent components (bones, muscles, organs, tissues, etc.) both grossly and microscopically (anatomy, neuroanatomy, histology, cellular biology); how the body, and all of its constituent components, functions under normal conditions (physiology, biochemistry, biophysics, behavior); the role and place of nature and/or the environment in the normal or abnormal development of the structure and function of the body, and its constituent components (genetics, microbiology); how the body, and all of its components, functions under abnormal conditions such as illness, disease, injury, congenital defects, stress (pathology, bacteriology); the effect on the body, and its constituent parts, of various medications and chemicals (pharmacology).

In an also oversimplified description, <u>the clinical sciences</u> consist of information to be taught to and learned by the medical student about the causes (etiology), signs and symptoms (complaints), diagnoses, diagnostic procedures, prognosis (outcome), natural course and treatment of the spectrum of medical and surgical conditions which are found in the human (disease, illness, defects, injuries, infections, etc).

Meyer Sonis M.D.

Built on the foundations of the information from the basic and clinical sciences, the medical student develops skills and gains practice experience in applying this information. The medical student learns to: secure a medical history from a patient and/or his/her family (interviewing a patient); conduct a physical examination and performing various clinical procedures (taking blood, giving injections, doing a spinal tap, etc.), at first on fellow medical students or plastic replicas of a human body and then on patients under supervision of a medical educator; gain skills in applying information to a variety of patients while rotating on a scheduled basis through all of the various clinical specialties or subspecialties (such as Anesthesiology, Internal Medicine, Pediatrics, Family Practice, Obstetrics, Psychiatry, Surgery, Cardiac Surgery).

The 125 approved medical schools in the United States are distributed throughout the geographic area of the country, with some states having several schools, some states one, some states none (Alaska, Delaware, Idaho, Wyoming, Montana). The operation of medical schools has become big business, as reflected in the 30 billion dollar annual income of all medical schools (estimated in 1990). Almost all of the approved medical schools operate as a private not-for-profit corporation or as a public not-for- profit organization. A very few medical schools, due to their financial debt and encumbrances, have developed affiliations with the large, powerful private for-profit health provider corporations or are operated as for profit medical schools (Caribbean). Over half of the current medical schools in the United States are known as State schools, because they receive a subsidy from their particular state in return for which they are obligated to give preference to acceptance of an applicant who is a resident of the state and is as qualified as other accepted applicants. Of the income earned by all of the medical schools, 4% is generated from tuition income while almost 35% to 50% is generated by the clinical practice of their full time faculty for which a fee is charged (i.e. patient care).

Skeletons in the Medical Closet
A Personal Story and a Professional Report

The proportion of income which is generated for the medical schools by the clinical practice of their full time medical faculty has been increasing during the past decade. This trend reflects the increased amount of time which medical school faculty as well as residents, interns, medical students, are devoting to direct patient care in the hospitals and outpatient services which are operated by or affiliated with the medical school. This clinical practice income is generated by payment for clinical care by third party payors (Medicare, Medicaid, BC/BS, Aetna, etc.) and benefits both the medical school (which receives a percentage of this clinical income from full time faculty) and the faculty (who are thus able to increase their earnings beyond salary). The quid pro quo in this mutual benefit system between the medical school and clinical faculty is the provision to the full time faculty by the medical school of an excellent benefit package plan (retirement, vacation, insurance) as well as office/equipment/secretarial/nursing staff/laboratory, at no cost to the physician. Of the 6000 hospitals in the United States, 100 of them are owned and operated by a medical school while 950 are affiliated with but not owned by a medical school.

More than ever before in the lifetime of our American medical schools, they have come under intense scrutiny, criticism and pressure regarding the need for reform in medical education, such as, curriculum, format, methods of teaching, admission procedures for acceptance of medical students, ability to monitor itself or the outcome of medical education. In addition, under the pressure of market place economics of medical practice, medical schools are being forced to examine their fiscal environment in order to survive. In support of the need for reform in medical education there have been a wealth of studies, some examples of which follow.

In a recent study (1991) of 1300 medical educators (and which included deans of medical schools) a majority of them indicated that "fundamental changes" are needed in medical education if medical students are to be "exposed to an appropriate range of patient problems." In a study of senior medical students (1990, 1991) a majority of them indicated that they received inadequate instruction on practice management, cost effective medical practice, nutrition, preventative care, patient follow-up, the socio-economic and emotional problems of patients. In a study (1991) utilizing a performance assessment test of senior medical students it was reported that: "20% of them were never supervised by an experienced teacher while they performed a history and physical examination of a patient; 11% of them reported being observed once by their supervisor; serious variability was found between students in their clinical competency." In yet another study (1990) of the performance of medical students it was reported that 60% to 90% of them did not wash their hands prior to or after conducting a physical examination in order to minimize infection transmission, 26% made errors in detecting heart murmurs, 61% made errors in examination of a swollen knee.

As a consequence of this criticism of and pressure on medical schools, certain directions of reform seem to be sufficiently clear as to gain the support of most medical educators. These medical education reforms were viewed as requiring: a greater emphasis on the development of the attitudes and skills that will sustain a lifetime of continuing learning by physicians; more attention to independent problem solving; greater integration of basic sciences and clinical sciences; more clinical education in ambulatory and community settings and less in hospital settings; a development of a system for more effective evaluation of medical educators and for rewarding excellence in medical educators. Even though changes for the better have taken place there remains high resistance to such change because the various clinical departments of a medical school have become so large and preoccupied with research/postgraduate medical education/generating clinical income so that undergraduate medical education has become a fifth wheel.

Medical Educators

Medical educators, that is "teachers" of undergraduate medical education (medical school) and/or of postgraduate medical education (interns, residents), are not "teachers" in the strict sense of the word, namely, persons who have been taught the science and art of pedagogy. Rather or instead they are physicians and basic scientists who have acquired the knowledge and skill of the basic and clinical sciences of medical education and who have chosen a career as a self designated medical teacher.

Some of these medical educators are full time salaried employees of a medical school and/or teaching hospital and are referred to as full time academic faculty; some are part time salaried employees of a medical school and/or teaching hospital and are referred to as part time academic faculty; some are not employees of a medical school or teaching hospital and are referred to as volunteer (i.e. no compensation) academic faculty, who contribute their time and services. All of these medical educators, in similar fashion as all other university or college teachers, are given an academic title (rank) in the medical school ranging from Instructor to Assistant Professor, to Associate Professor, to Professor, to Distinguished Professor, and are so designated according to criteria established for each rank by the specific medical school/university. Usually full time faculty are those who have embarked on a career in academic medicine and are promoted upward in rank and salary if they meet the established criteria for a particular rank, and some are promoted ultimately to tenure (i.e. permanent employment). Usually volunteer faculty are those who contribute their time and service in return for the "prestige" of the title and rank they hold.

For more than a generation, America's schools of medicine have been dominated by their full time faculty, who from time immemorial have been expected to devote their efforts to medical research, medical education and lastly to clinical practice with patients at their own institutions (hospitals and clinics). This was a model of "academe" which emulated European schools of medicine and medical educators. As funds for the increasing research efforts of full time faculty in U.S. medical schools and hospitals began to decrease, full time faculty began to devote an increasing amount of their time to "seeing" patients via "clinical practice plans" in order to generate income.

As per data available for 1996, there were approximately: 100,000 full time faculty, with 20% teaching the basic sciences and 80% teaching the clinical sciences in our medical schools; 148,000 volunteer faculty with 25% teaching in the basic sciences and 95% teaching in the clinical sciences in our medical schools. Some of these medical educators are primarily oriented to the conduct of research, so that the teaching of medical students and the supervision of residents takes second or third place in their interest. Others are primarily oriented to their clinical practice and the income generated, so that teaching may become secondary. Still others are heavily oriented and committed to teaching and this serves as their primary task. Most volunteer medical educators are physicians who are primarily in the private sector of clinical practice (independent of medical school/ hospital) and who contribute their time as a teacher of medical students and supervisor of residents in exchange for the prestige and status of an academic faculty appointment and the opportunity of continued learning. Medical educators, as expected, vary in their abilities to teach and to serve as positive role models for the physicians to be. Some medical educators view everything in dogmatic terms so that they brook no questions or discussions from students. Some medical educators epitomize the expression "do what I say not what I practice" and have little time for the learning curve of their students and some become the recipients of student awards for teaching and for responding to the needs of a "learner." In general, as can be surmised, medical education and educators are a mixed bag of blessings and curses. It is

Skeletons in the Medical Closet
A Personal Story and a Professional Report

within this mix of medical educators that the "novice" physician learns, makes mistakes, requires nurturing of his or her emerging responsibility for patient care.

It is this group of physicians called medical educators who have a responsibility for aiding the novice to become more "tuned in" on patient education, patient courtesy and patient safety, the risks of invasive procedures if conducted without adequate training, and the vulnerability of patients to unnecessary procedures.

Medical Students

At the present time there are about 65,000 students enrolled in 125 schools of medicine in the United States. Thus an average of 500+ students in each of the schools and an average of 100+ students in each of the four year curriculum to become a doctor. From the aggregate of all medical schools about 15,000 new physicians are graduated each year to become part of the existing physician workforce pool.

During the past two or three decades there has been a great deal of controversy on the matter of whether the United States has or will have an over or under supply of physicians to serve the needs of the population in the United States. Some studies have suggested and projected an oversupply of physicians which in turn was believed would increase competition, drive cost down, and "move" physicians to physician shortage areas. This projection did not occur. Other studies have suggested that there will be a shortage of physicians if equal access to medical care is provided to all population groups. This projection is as yet unanswered.

More recently this controversy has been fueled by the emphasis on cost containment of health services and thus containment of physician fees which comprise 20% to 25% of health service expenditures. A consensus of opinion now exists which suggests that by the year 2000 there will be a surplus

(60% more than needed) of specialists and a balance between the supply and requirements for primary care physicians. All in all, this issue of an over or under supply of physicians may ultimately be settled not by the question of how many physicians do we require but by the question of how many physicians can we afford?

During this 30 years in which this controversy regarding an over or under supply of physicians took place, the number of students seeking to become a physician was in a state of flux. In the 1970's this number reached an all time high, namely 5 applicants for every medical school slot available; in the 1980's the number of applicants/available slot decreased; in the 1990's this downward trend is only now beginning to become reversed, namely 2 to 3 applicants for every slot. This decrease of applicants has been explained in a variety of ways, such as: the increasing cost of medical education; the possibility of income limits (cost containment) on physician income; the financial attraction of other professions; the disillusionment with the "ideals" of becoming a physician; the fear of incurring a large debt (now over $60,000) in order to pay for the cost of a medical education. Added to this are the factors of discouragement experienced by an applicant consequent to the fact that medical schools accept half or less than half of the applicants.

Despite the years of experience which medical schools have amassed in selecting students for admission to become a physician, there has been no sure fire method or criteria found to accurately predict the characteristics of an applicant which can lead them to become a "compleat physician," namely, a superb clinical scientist who is completely comfortable with the human relationship aspect of patient care, and who can morally and ethically balance their self interests and public good. The predominant profile characteristics of applicants who were admitted to the medical schools during the past few years were applicants: with a college grade point average of 3.4 (based on a 4.0 point scale); possessing a baccalaureate degree in the

Skeletons in the Medical Closet
A Personal Story and a Professional Report

sciences; who were more science oriented than people focused, more competitive than cooperative, more comfortable as soloists than as a team member, more egocentric than other related, more conservative in their politics. It should be noted that admitted applicants to medical schools also reflected the trend of the increasing acceptance of female applicants (30% - 50% of applicants), and minority students (20%). This is a far cry from the "quota" system regarding acceptance of minority students as medical students which was quietly in use prior to World War II.

There is no doubt of the fact that the four year experience of becoming a physician places a significant amount of internal and external demands on the medical student. Not only have these students placed themselves in the position of having to acquire and apply an inordinate amount of information but they also have placed themselves in a situation of needing to postpone or curtail or limit or control the developmental drives and goals ordinarily posed for young adults between the ages of 22 to 30. I am referring to the developmental objectives for this age group of: becoming independent of their family financially, socially, emotionally; earning their own income as the basis for their economic security; developing mature social and sexual relationships; considering or initiating steps towards marriage and their own family. In addition to placing a "hold" on these developmental objectives, the young adult who chooses to become a physician enters into a four year life experience not ordinarily experienced by young adults. I am referring to the experiences for a young adult, such as, the dissection of a human body, performing autopsies, physically examining and touching another person while not becoming personally and/or sexually involved, making your first/ second/third correct diagnosis and making your first/ second/third serious mistake, the death of your first patient, performing your first spinal tap. I am referring to the four year experience of molding a young adult into a professional person who can assume responsibility for the life of another person, can be self critical, can place another person's interests above his/her own personal interests. I am referring to the "learning culture" of novice physicians which inculcates the myth of infallibility of the physician while stimulating the need to "hide" your mistakes.

In addition to these developmental pressures on a medical student there is the pressure of the debt incurred to pay for the privilege of becoming a physician. In 1996 the average debt of a medical student on graduation from medical school was approximately $50,000 to $60,000 and an increase of 77% since 1980. The cost in 1997 of a medical school education (i.e. to pay for tuition and fees) ranged from $2,300/year to $50,000/year depending on the type of medical school (private/high status/public). Since 1960 tuition at state supported medical schools has risen by 200%, while tuition at private schools has risen by 400%. Concern about this economic burden on medical students has led to serious questions on the matter of whether this was pushing medical students away from lower income producing practices into higher income producing medical specialties in order to pay off this debt.

It can be said that most medical students are able to withstand the personal and economic pressures. However, as per data available, some medical students cannot make it so that some withdraw or are dismissed, take a leave of absence or repeat a school year (i.e. 6% to 7%), some have been reported as suffering from an alcohol and drug problem (4%), some have been reported with AIDS (14%). Of the 125 approved schools of medicine, over 60% have a policy regarding students with substance abuse problems, suggesting the major problem this does pose.

Physician Generalists and Specialists

Of all of the physicians who may comprise The Physician Industry approximately 80%to 85% (600,000) directly provide clinical care to patients as a physician generalist or specialist.

In the United States, a physician, upon receipt of his Medical Degree or Osteopathic Degree and completion of an approved internship and securing of a medical license, can designate himself or herself as a generalist or specialist physician regardless of whether he or she has been specifically trained for a specialty through formal postgraduate medical education and training. In a study reported in 1987, it was found that 12% of physicians listed as physician specialists in the Boston telephone directory were not listed in the formal records of that specialty. Since World War II the number of these self designated physician specialists in the United States has been steadily decreasing as a consequence of the aging of the medical profession, the emergence and growth of specialty medicine and surgery (in keeping with advances in our medical and surgical knowledge), the increased attention to formal credentials set by standard setting medical organizations and hospitals. In most cases these self designated physician specialists (now estimated at 30% of all specialists) tend to be physicians who graduated medical school prior to 1960 and whose knowledge of and skill in the specialty was gained as a result primarily of experience alone.

As one would surmise the characteristics of their clinical practice differs between generalist and specialist physicians. Several studies have illustrated this. In a study reported in 1960, but whose findings are still valid today, it was found that over 50% of the outpatient visits of patients to generalist physicians were for problems associated with up to twenty different diagnoses, while over 50% of the outpatient visits of patients to specialist physicians were for problems associated with up to six different diagnoses. In yet another study (1988) it was reported that general family practitioners and pediatricians spent more time on average with patients (3+ patients/hour) than internists/surgeons did, and that (as expected) psychiatrists spent the most time with a patient (1.5 patients/hour). Additional features of differences between generalists and specialists have been reported, such as, income level tends to be higher for specialists, specialists tend to order more clinical tests and procedures, specialists tend to make more referrals of patients to other physicians, specialists tend to see more patients with chronic medical disorders.

Standards for Postgraduate Medical Education

With the establishment of standards by the American Medical Association in 1910 to guide medical school education it would follow that ultimately standards would be developed by which to guide post graduate medical education. At first, standards were established for monitoring the teaching hospitals which served as a base for the internship experience of medical school graduates; and then in an incremental fashion, from 1910 onward, post graduate medical education program standards were developed and monitored for all of the current twenty-five different medical and surgical specialties.

These post graduate education standards have been hand tailored by each physician specialty and subspecialty to fit their own requirements regarding the knowledge and skill needed to practice that specialty. These standards serve as guidelines for the various post graduate medical education programs in the "teaching hospitals." The scope of these guidelines range from information about the content which must be taught and learned, to the number and types of patients to be seen, to the number and kinds of clinical procedures which must be performed, to the scope of clinical problems to be encountered, to the number of autopsies to be performed, to the number and kind of formal educational programs available (seminars, literature, patient conferences, etc.), to the amount and kind of supervision to be provided, to the records of "formal evaluation" of the trainee. These accreditation standards utilized by the various specialty authorities have been made meaningful because of their universal acceptance by local/ state/ national governments as the basis for licensing of practitioners or hospitals and by third party payors as the basis for reimbursement criteria.

During the past thirty years there has been a marked trend in the training and production of specialists over generalists. This trend has been of serious concern to those responsible for planning the fiscal future of health care delivery, since it is estimated that the number of physician specialists and sub-specialists now exceed the number required as compared with the number of generalist physicians required. As a consequence of steps taken to slow this trend by utilization of the flow of governmental funds, it is reported that from 1991 through 1996 there has been a 170% increase in generalist specialty certification, and a 33% decrease in medical specialty certification. However, it must also be borne in mind that the past increased trend in producing physician specialists was in keeping with the ever expanding base of knowledge in the medical sciences and clinical services.

At the present time there are 7000 postgraduate medical education programs for training in a physician specialty or sub-specialty. These programs are located in only 1500 teaching hospitals of the 6000 hospitals in the United States. There are approximately 98,000 "trainees" in these programs, with almost half of these trainees located in only 100 of these teaching hospitals (primarily located in the Northeast region of the United States). Of these 98,000 "trainees," 40% of them were in the specialties of Medicine, Pediatrics, Family Practice, while 60% of them were in the specialty of Surgery and its subspecialties.

Since World War II the professional career track for a physician, upon completion of medical school, has undergone major changes which have favored training in the medical/

surgical specialties and sub-specialties and de-emphasized general practice. Prior to World War II every senior medical student had to enter and complete a two year program of internship at any teaching hospital if they were ultimately to be eligible for a medical license. It was during this time that the novice physician not only could gain the experience required but also have time to decide on his/her next career choice, either to practice as a general practitioner or negotiate with a teaching hospital to become a resident in a physician specialty or subspecialty. Parenthetically it should be noted that it was from this pre-World War II group of physicians that the general practitioner and self-designated physician specialist emerged. As a consequence of the increased need for physicians in the Armed Services during WWII internships were decreased to nine months time and post-graduate education for specialty training was also decreased in its length of time. From that point to the present, changes have been made in the standards and format for internships and residences.

Currently a senior medical student participates in a formal matching plan (voluntarily agreed upon by medical schools and approved hospitals) in which a central authority (under auspices of a National Accrediting Authority) matches the application choice of a senior medical student against the choices of the hospitals to which the student has applied (first, second and third choice of student matched against first, second and third choice of hospital). Though the novice physician upon completion of medical school now enters a specialty track, the track is set up to enable the novice to complete only one year of training now called Post Graduate Year One (PGY1) (formerly the internship year) and leave or continue to completion of the required number of years (PGY2, PGY3, PGY4) designated by the particular specialty. This tends however to push the novice toward a specialty. Some physician specialties require three years of training (i.e. Family Practice, Medicine, Pediatrics) while some require five or more years of training (Thoracic Surgery,

Neurological Surgery). Following upon successful completion of the specialty training program the physician specialist is now designated as "Board Eligible," meaning, as eligible to take the certification examination given by the appropriate specialty board (such as, the American Board of Internal Medicine, American Board of Pediatrics, etc.). The physician specialist of the particular "Specialty" on successful passage of the written and oral examination, is now designated as "Board Certified." Physicians who are Board Eligible may elect not to take the certification examination for a variety of reasons (fear of failing, insufficient opportunity or time to prepare, do not believe this is of value) but nevertheless they can practice their specialty and call themselves specialist; physicians who fail their certification examination can repeat the examination several times and can continue their practice.

Prior to World War II some hospitals paid a small stipend to their interns and residents. This was not a salary since they were not counted as employees of the hospital. More prestigious hospitals did not pay a stipend but gave their interns and residents an allowance for housing, food and uniforms. Currently a PGY1 resident (equivalent to intern) receives a salary, and thus is an employee of a hospital, which averages $21,000. per year plus room and board, and in return maintains a heavy work schedule of 60 to 80 hours per week. As a physician continues in his/her postgraduate training beyond PGY1 his/her salary is increased incrementally from PGY2 to completion.

In assuming the responsibility for postgraduate medical education programs, and the 98,000 residents currently in these programs, teaching hospitals have also assumed the costs of operating these programs, namely expenses such as salary/fringe benefit/room and board of the resident, faculty supervision, managerial costs. These costs are then passed by the hospital through a per diem rate for each hospitalized patient. Because costs of teaching hospitals are greater than non-teaching hospitals (due to costs of post-graduate education) reimbursement rates of third party payors are higher.

Throughout the period of time during which postgraduate medical education has evolved to its current scope, valid concerns and criticisms have been leveled at the methods and manner by which our teaching hospitals educate, train, develop and monitor the "trainee" physician specialists. These concerns have been enunciated by physicians themselves, the public consumer, and the third party payors and have basically asked the questions of whether such methods assure the public of physician specialists who are competent, ethical, cost effective and skillful in their rendering of medical care.

Though these criticisms and concerns are valid and do require attention, there is no surefire way by which all incompetent and unethical physician specialists can be weeded out/identified in advance. This does not mean that all is hopeless but it does mean that the medical profession as a whole must be constantly refining and upgrading its methods for selection, education, training and evaluation of physician specialists. Through the higher rate of reimbursement for hospital care of a patient in a teaching hospital, the federal government has estimated that this subsidy of teaching hospitals is costing the government an average of $70,000/year for each resident in training. For this reason many non-teaching hospital have been outraged, and have been seeking more parity with the teaching hospital or have moved to an affiliation with a teaching hospital. More recently, the federal government has been requesting and conducting serious financial audits of teaching hospitals, medical schools and universities because of expenditures which are difficult to justify such as charging frills, entertainment to research/teaching grant and because of the "double dipping" of teaching hospitals, such as, billing for services rendered by a "resident trainee" and billing for the same service by the faculty medical educator supervisor.

Skeletons in the Medical Closet
A Personal Story and a Professional Report

It has become evident that our physicians, in becoming physicians and physician specialists, were primarily learning about hospitalized patients who: were sicker and manifested more chronic problems; posed more complex diagnostic and treatment problems; and who required more high-tech procedures, as opposed to the average medical and surgical problems of patients seeking medical care. It has also become evident that with the changes in hospitals (such as, shorter length of stays, increase in the volume of patients and procedures) the "trainee" specialist has been placed under pressure to see more patients per unit of time with less and less opportunity to spend time with patients and/or follow the patient over a period of time. As a consequence, traditional training programs have begun consideration of broadening the sites for and content of training to include the more ordinary problems of patients, as found in ambulatory settings.

As a means of increasing the requirements for a physician specialist to constantly update his/her knowledge and skill, steps have been instituted by various medical authorities to require periodic reexamination and recertification of physician specialists, instead of granting them a onetime lifetime certification. Unfortunately only some of the specialties have done so (Family Practice, Cardiology) while the other specialties have been dragging their feet. As it became clear that some physician specialists were not sufficiently trained in the various procedures which they perform, increasing attention has been given to the need for stricter delineation by a hospital of the clinical privilege granted to a physician on their staff. With the increased recognition by medical educators of the variations in knowledge and skill between physician specialist "trainees" within the same program or between different programs, various steps have been taken to develop measures for assessing clinical skills of novice physicians. With the more public scrutiny of adverse events occurring to hospitalized patients, increasing attention is now being focused on the mistakes which trainees do make, on the environment of teaching which makes it difficult for a trainee to admit to such mistakes and seek help, and on the imperative need for more diligent supervision of trainees by medical educators. In a subsequent Chapter more details will be presented regarding the question of who watches the doctors and hospitals in order to monitor the safety, competence and quality of medical care which is rendered.

Income, Expenses and Fees of Physicians and Who Pays

Before proceeding with this section I believe that I must reveal my own bias as a physician regarding physician income, fees and expenses so that this bias does not get in the way of my reporting the factual information which is available. I am of the mind, and I have continued to be of this mind during almost fifty years of being a physician, that being a physician is a very rewarding way of earning a comfortable living. By rewarding, I am referring to the satisfaction of serving others while enjoying the challenge of this work and getting paid for it to boot. By a comfortable living I am referring to generating an income which enables my family and me to live comfortably while receiving the respect of others. Though, in the past, I found as a medical educator that there was a wide disparity between the income and tax benefits available to a physician in the profit sector of medical care as compared to the full time medical educator, this disparity has been greatly lessened. Unfortunately, I believe that the climate of the corporate executive world with its bottom line of profit has infiltrated the personal and professional world of all physicians. Despite the complaints of physicians regarding the excess amount of paperwork, the bureaucratic maze of third party payors, the burdens of patient care, the limits on income, and the increasing costs of liability insurance, I still would tell young people that becoming a physician is a very rewarding way to earn a comfortable living.

Skeletons in the Medical Closet
A Personal Story and a Professional Report

Having now shared my bias I will proceed to reporting the information which is available and published on physician income.

In reporting on this information it must be remembered that information about income is a very private matter, not just for physicians but for others as well. For this reason published information about physician income, fees and expenses are not based on a nose by nose count of physicians and their fiscal records. The only probable place such comparatively accurate fiscal information would be available, if any place, is in the records at the Internal Revenue Service. In most publications of information on physician income, fees and expenses, the information is secured by various organization (i.e., American Medical Association, American Association of Medical Colleges, Medical Economics Inc., third party payors) through questionnaires which physicians are requested to complete (with or without signature, providing ranges and not actual amounts) and/or special studies via sampling methods; and/or through the data which a third party payor collects for physician reimbursement (Medicare, Blue Cross/Blue Shield, insurance companies). In keeping with these general methods of securing information and the limited information available, the data and information provided by me is aggregate, average or median data, which may not be comparable from one source of information to another.

To begin with, despite the "bad press" given physicians and despite the various disclaimers of physicians, physicians are still the most highly compensated of all professions, though they are being pushed by the legal profession. Further all physicians are not equal in the amount of income they generate and receive, i.e., surgeons earn more than their non-surgical colleagues, internists earn more than general practitioners/family practitioners, some receive cash/some receive checks, etc. It has been projected that from 1980 to the year 2000 there will be major shifts in patterns of practice style of physicians, income generated, and in the source of income to physicians. For example, the proportion of total income to physicians will shift increasingly to Federal and third party payors and less from the patient themselves. Recently, for example, Medicare reported that for physicians who serve Medicare patients an average of 70% of their income is based on Medicare payments.

In 1990 the distribution of net income (after deducting professional expenses but before taxes) for all office based physicians (not hospital or medical school based) was as follows: 15% earned an annual income of $80,000 or less; 30% earned an annual income between $80,000 to $150,000; 35% earned an annual income between $150,000 to $300,000; 8% earned an annual income over $300,000. In 1990, the median income had risen to $155,000. In 1997: general practitioners were reported with a gross income of $152,000 and $86,640 in net earnings; psychiatrists were reported with a gross income of $165,000 and a net income of $113,000; neurosurgeons were reported with a gross income of $500,000 and a net income of $288,000. In general, during the period of 1990 to 1997, the net income for surgical specialties remained higher than for non-surgical specialties, and the income increase of physicians continued to exceed the inflation rate.

The median net income of physicians also varied between regions, with the highest in the South Atlantic states. Physicians in urban areas earned more than those in rural areas; physicians who have been in practice longer earn more up until their 25th to 30th year of practice; physicians who are older in age earn more until they reach about 60 years of age. Physicians who are incorporated earn more than unincorporated physicians. It is of interest to note, though the data is not usually reported in this manner, that in 1990 the profit margin for all categories of specialists who are office based ranged from 46% to 60%, which by all standards in business is a very good return on the cost of doing business.

Skeletons in the Medical Closet
A Personal Story and a Professional Report

In all fairness to physicians and the view of physicians as being "overpaid," there have been various studies which have attempted to compare physician's income to other professional groups. Each of these studies have had limits to their validity or comparability. During World War II (and based on one such study) the federal government decided that officers who were physicians should be paid an extra bonus over their equivalent line officers, in order to compensate them for the additional cost of their education. In a more recent study, reported in 1994, it was concluded that for primary care physicians the financial return on the cost of their education and their working hours was poorer than that of a physician specialist or a business profession or an attorney or dentist. For example, in this same study, the annual cash flow per hour (income minus cost divided by hours worked) for primary care physicians was the lowest as compared to the other professions (procedure based physician specialists, dentistry, law, business), while procedure based physician specialists received the highest cash flow over all others, but at age 55 to 65 years lawyers received the highest.

In conjunction with the income earned by physicians, some physicians increase their income by ownership or investment in clinical laboratories and /or pharmaceutical companies, health care facilities (for-profit hospitals, clinics, managed care companies). For example, in 1988, a clinical laboratory was owned by 5% of all physician generalists, 9% of all physician specialists, 12% of all surgeons, 9% of physicians in solo practice in comparison to 13% of physicians in group practice. Medicare studies have shown that 45% more laboratory studies are ordered by physicians who own or invest in a clinical laboratory than do physicians who do not. Because of this conflict of interest, legislation has been enacted to monitor and curb this conflict of interest.

In reviewing this information about the income for physicians, a special mention must be made of the income of physicians who are full time faculty members of a medical school/ teaching hospital (medical educators). In 1996 the mean annual income for a full time academic physician ranged from $96,000 for an instructor to $133,000 for an assistant professor, to $161,000 for an associate professor, to $190,000 for a professor to $290,000 for a department chairman. This is exclusive of supplemental income generated by their own clinical practice, of the income equivalent of their fringe benefit package, of "free" office space, support staff (nurses, secretaries), laboratory equipment provided by the medical school/teaching hospital.

On the matter of the professional expenses which the physician incurs most of the information available is about physicians in office based practice. The information which is available for physicians in hospital or medical school practice (as commented on above) is surmised, namely that their professional expenses are much less (if at all) than their office based colleagues because of the perquisites/fringe benefits available to them. Ordinarily the professional expenses of office based physicians are legitimate tax deductible business expenses against the gross income of the physicians. These deductible business expenses can include: office expense (i.e., rent/mortgage for office space, telephone, utilities, business equipment, etc.); non-physician salaries including fringe benefits (secretary, receptionist, nurse, technicians, etc.); medical supplies (x-ray films, chemicals, antiseptics); depreciation/lease of medical equipment (EKG machine, clinical laboratory equipment, x-ray, etc.); medical liability insurance; transportation (parking, garage), business travel, entertainment, charitable contributions, books/ journals needed for medical practice, professional dues; interest on loans. Also expenses such as follows can be legitimately deducted, if documented, as business expense: a part of mortgage/ utilities etc. of a physician's own home or building, if office space is provided; rental or purchase of a car utilized for business; or employment of a family member as a non-physician employee. As with income, the professional expenses of office based physicians varies between specialists, geographic regions, ages of physicians, length of time in practice, kind of practice (solo, group or incorporated).

Up until the need for cost containment measures were instituted by Medicare (and third party payors), the fee charged by a physician for his or her services was totally under the control of the physician. The fee which the physician set was usually based on the prevailing fee charged by other similar physicians in a given geographic area. In other words, the fee charged was based on the free marketplace and competition in a given community. For this reason the term coined to describe this fee setting practice was "the usual customary fee in the given community for the type of physician rendering the service.." For example, and on a personal note, at the time (1947): when I "moonlighted" for several general practitioners in a "labor" class community, the fee charged for an office visit was $5.00 (1947) plus the cost of simple laboratory studies.done in the office and the time allotted by these practitioners for a routine office visit was 10 minutes; with my specialty practice of pediatric psychiatry (1950), the usual fee for a 50 minute office visit was $25.00.

To meet the increased cost of medical services, Medicare in 1985 spark plugged <u>the first major change in the traditional basis for physician fee setting in a competitive marketplace.</u> This change was based on the introduction of a standardized "resource-based relative value scale" (RBRVS) into fee reimbursement. In arriving at this scale several factors were taken into consideration, such as the amount of time devoted to patient contact, the time utilized by the physician pre and post services rendered (report reading, consultation with referring source, report/record keeping), the intensity per unit of time for performing the services (mental effort, technical skill, knowledge required), practice costs, cost of education to become a specialist. Though this RBRVS in its creation was viewed as a more equitable alternative to a fee for service payment system, it nevertheless has had to be periodically modified to make it more equitable to physicians. In addition to this initial major change in the basis for setting of fees for physician services introduced by third party payors, there has been a progression of third party payors initiatives aimed at harnessing the costs of physician services introduced, such as a capitation method of pre-payment, standardizing the cost of a specific procedure, bargaining for discounts with physician groups. At the present time third party payors have established a fee scale for almost 7,000 procedures but as yet there has been no sure method found for fee setting of physician services which can insulate medical decisions from physician income.

In concluding this chapter on The Physician Industry, it must be noted that the industry itself is well aware of the major changes it will be facing in the next decade. Some of these changes have become necessary because of the changing nature of the population in our country; some of these changes have become necessary because of the scientific advances which are being made in our understanding of medical problems and their solutions; some of these changes have become necessary because of the slowness by which the organizations of the medical profession accept new directions; some of these changes have become necessary because of the inability of physicians to come to grips with the equation of private gain and public responsibility; some of these changes have become necessary because of the increased awareness that medical care at times is not safe, is not competent, is not effective, is not in keeping with standards of quality. Finally, and most important, some of these changes have become necessary because of the pressures on the industry posed by the public consumer of medical care, who are demanding that physicians must become better listeners and better talkers since studies have confirmed that most patients never get to tell their whole story and most physicians spend little time on educating patients.

CHAPTER FIVE

THE HOSPITAL INDUSTRY

The hospital industry is also a major component of the medical-industrial complex in the United States. Though the hospital industry includes hospitals, nursing homes, skilled nursing homes, hospices, rehabilitation centers, ambulatory and home health care services, the primary focus of this chapter will be on that of the hospital itself.

From information available, it is estimated (at the present time) that during the course of a year approximately 10 to 20 percent of the total population in the United States become hospitalized patients, or the equivalent of 22 to 40 million patients. For some hospitalized patients the experience may be a fortunate one, in that the food is good, served warm and in a timely manner, the hospital personnel are courteous and responsive to the patient's needs, and the medical complaints which brought the patient to the hospital are resolved without complications. For other patients the experience in the hospital may not be as fortunate, not because of poor food or uncomfortable surroundings or discourteous personnel since this will not kill the patient, but because of unexpected complications, unanticipated problems, medication errors, unnecessary procedures, unwarranted surgery, accidents or errors of omission or commission.

In 1990 there were approximately 6,000 community hospitals (excluding government hospitals) into which the millions of patients were admitted. Because hospitals have not been planned for generally according to a rational plan of supply and demand, some communities do not have a hospital, while some geographic areas have more hospitals than others, ranging for example from a high of 7.6 beds for every 1,000 persons in Washington D.C. to 3.2 beds for every 1,000 persons in

Meyer Sonis M.D.

Vermont. In 1990 these millions of patients admitted to hospitals generated approximately 200 to 300 billion dollars in income for these hospitals as well as providing employment to over 3 to 4 million people. In 1990, of every dollar spent in the United States on personal health services, 44 cents were spent on hospital care, 23 cents on physicians, 7 cents on dentists, 4 cents on other professional services, 9 cents on nursing home care, 7 cents on medication and medical supplies, 5 cents on other items. By any criteria this is big business, and has remained so to the present despite cost cutting and down sizing.

The Emergence of the Modern Hospital in the United States

Even though today's hospital continues to bear a resemblance to its predecessor hospital of yesterday, the modern hospital of today (1999) is a far cry from the hospital of only 20 to 30 years ago, let alone the hospital of 50 to 200 years ago.

At the time of the first hospital census, in 1873, it was reported that there were 178 hospitals in the United States. By 1900, 800 hospitals were in operation. By 1990, this had grown to over 6,000 hospitals. In early America the hospital was primarily an almshouse, operated as a charitable institution for the homeless, disabled poor and infirm and served as a shelter for persons with contagious diseases during epidemics. Most ailing persons, who were not indigent, were cared for in their home by their physician and only went to the hospital, if needed, to die. By 1900, as a consequence of advances in antisepsis, cleanliness and anesthetic agents, as well as the emergence of the profession of nursing, hospitals became medical facilities wherein surgeons began to admit their private patients for surgery (not just the poor). Some of these hospitals were holdovers of the earlier hospitals for the disabled poor and infirm. Some of these hospitals were established as private clinics and owned and operated by a physician or surgical practitioner. Some of these hospitals became the forerunners of the hospitals which emerged during the period of 1900 to 1950 namely: a medical facility:

- which would provide lodging, food, medical, nursing and other care for the medically and surgically sick;
- which would serve all classes of population;
- which for the most part was established as a private non-profit organization under the governance of a lay Board of Trustees, but operated by given physicians who were the medical staff entitled to admit and care for patients:
- which received payment for hospitalization services through patient fees which were underwritten by some form of private hospital insurance (by 1940 there were 87 different private hospital insurance plans, including Blue Cross);
- which would, on a voluntary basis, maintain accreditation standards established and periodically reviewed by the Joint Commission on Accreditation of Hospitals and the governmental authorities which license hospitals;
- which had a strong relationship to medical education, whereby the hospital served as a "practice site" for medical students, interns, and the specialty training of residents.

Thus emerged the rudimentary model of our modern hospital. The evolution of the American hospital differed from the evolution of the European hospital in one major way - the mode of payment for hospital services. In the European model, hospital payment was via a governmentally mandated insurance (in one form or another) or hospitals which were owned, operated and managed by the government; in the United States the mode of hospital payment had been private (such as from the patient or private insurance) until the advent of the Medicare program (governmentally mandated).

Meyer Sonis M.D.

Following upon the development of the rudimentary model of our modern hospital, the period after World War II (1950 to 1970) became the renaissance period for hospital development in the United States. Under the impetus of federal legislation, beginning in 1946, billions of dollars were made available for hospital construction, renovation and refurbishing. This enabled hospitals, for examples, to expand into rural and impoverished geographic areas, to modernize old physical plants, to prepare space for new equipment and services, to add space for physician offices, and to "think big" for example in terms of heliports/garages. Because of requirements imposed by federal legislation and regulations regarding government funding, an impetus was now given to the development of hospitals according to an organized, designed and rational plan for hospital construction/renovation/ expansion. This plan required it to be based on the results of an assessment of the need for a hospital/expansion of a hospital in a particular geographic area (i.e. demographic/epidemiological/clinical/population studies), collaboration with all pertinent state and local authorities and agencies, involvement of community persons. Additional legislation provided funds for a whole host of new initiatives such as: the extension of general hospitals into serving as a community health center (including beds for psychiatric patients); the utilization of hospitals as regional cancer, stroke and heart centers, focused on a regional geographic area; the establishment of clinical research centers in hospitals in order to advance our medical knowledge. Perhaps of greatest importance in the development of the modern hospital was the monumental legislation which for the first time in the United States mandated hospitals and related physician services for an entire population group, namely, the Medicare and Medicaid Program of 1965. In light of the initial objections of organized medicine to such federally mandated services, this legislation was finally able to be implemented by assuring hospitals and physicians that their services would be paid for at a rate set by them.

Skeletons in the Medical Closet
A Personal Story and a Professional Report

From this renaissance period the best and worst of times for our hospitals and medical care emerged, as well as the seeds for the current discontent with our hospitals and medical care in the United States.

It was during this period of time that scientific and technological advances enabled our hospitals to rely increasingly on high technology and procedures, but which brought with it mixed blessings. On the one hand, the increased utilization by physicians of this high technology, equipment and procedures of the modern hospital [such as Nuclear Magnetic Resonance (NMR), Computerized Axial Topography (CAT), Positive Emission Topography (PET), Cardiopulmonary Bypass Machines, Ultrasound and Lasers] has remarkably sharpened and transformed the ability of physicians to diagnose and treat our diseases, illnesses and injuries. Our hospitals were thus enabled to break new ground which was reflected in organ transplantation, salvage and repair of diseased hearts, breakup of kidney stones, and the development of intensive care units, but to mention a few. On the other hand, this progress has increased the cost of hospital care, introduced newer risks for patients, provoked competition between hospitals to have the newest of the new and unfortunately has stimulated unnecessary studies and procedures on patients.

It was also during this period of time, under pressure of cost containment, that hospitals underwent a transition from their role as a service institution to their role as a business organization, with its eye on the bottom line expenses. In following the dictates of this business approach some of the hospitals of today: attempt to fill as many of its beds as possible and maintain as high an occupancy rate as it can, while attempting to fill these beds with as many patients as possible who are able to pay for their care (self, third-party payors); maintain a policy vigilance on its fiscal break-even point; discourage admission of non-insured patients and/or patients with disease/illness/injuries which are costly to care for and which the patient or third party payor cannot pay; guard against excess labor costs (i.e., lower salaries, less fringe benefits, under-staffing/over-scheduling, untrained staff). Other hospitals of today employ various marketing tools to sell its product over a competitor hospital, such as: promoting its newest "laser" equipment for "painless" surgery, its gourmet kitchen, its special experts; encouraging utilization of its high technology equipment and procedures, for which there may be a higher income mark-up; providing incentives for its income-generating physicians such as subsidized office space, secretarial services, parking, malpractice insurance and other benefits; the promotion of various organizational arrangements aimed at increasing surplus income and lessening expenses, (i.e, consortium of several hospitals for mass purchasing or laundry services, contracting with various vendors for its housekeeping, maintenance, food and laboratory services, setting up "quasi" profit subsidiaries of its non-profit organization). One example of such "business" thinking was reported in a recently published book, which named one hospital which increased its revenue in one year by 33% through recruitment of a "superstar" open heart surgeon who did 400 procedures his first year and anticipated 1200 the next year.

It was also during this period of time that a mounting discontent with our hospitals manifested itself through the various pushes and pulls on our hospitals, physicians, and third-party payors. It is a discontent with: the ever increasing cost of hospital and medical service; the ever increasing gap in access of these services between the several economic and social classes in the United States; the continuing disparity in rates of disease, illness and death between various population segments in the United States; the mistakes and failures reported in our hospitals; the financial incentive structure for hospitals and physicians which supports the over utilization of high income procedures by physicians.

It is a discontent which has been expressed in various lay and consumer publications in articles on the crisis in health care

Skeletons in the Medical Closet
A Personal Story and a Professional Report

and health care insurance. These articles have lamented the fact that though the United States spends more on health care than other countries, the United States ranks lower than other countries in life expectancies, in percentage of babies born with inadequate birth weight (Bulgaria, Hong Kong, and the Soviet Union all do better), and in access to health care for all of their population.

As a consequence of these various pushes and pulls on hospitals during the past decade or two, and in response to the mounting discontent in our country with our hospitals and our health system, major changes were and are being posed for hospitals, physicians and the system of health care delivery in the United States. This need for change was and is reflected in the various alternatives under consideration, ranging from a total reorganization of the health system through a national health service to cover the total population to the partial changes instituted by Congress, such as in health maintenance organizations (HMO), managed care promotion, subsidization of select patient groups.

Yet to come, if at all, are changes which will forge a system of health care from our non-system so that we can address: the duplication, fragmentation and competing array of providers and suppliers of health and hospital services; the need for greater standardization and practice guidelines for hospital and medical practices and the increased monitoring of the outcome and effectiveness of such practices; the need for more effective centralization of accountability for services rendered; the development of a plan and system for physician compensation which is equitable and supportive of the patient doctor relationship; the need for patient education towards promoting an informed patient.

Meyer Sonis M.D.

Types and Categories of Hospitals

In order to enable comparisons to be made between hospitals, hospitals in the United States have been categorized or classified in a variety of ways, such as the number of beds, percentage of bed occupancy, patient populations served, services offered, number and kind of employees, income and expenses, mortality rates, procedures performed.

One such means of classifying hospitals is by the average length of stay of a patient in a hospital, taking into consideration all patients and all the medical and surgical problems of all of these patients and all of the various factors which can influence the length of time a patient remains in the hospital. Thus, some hospitals are classified as short-term hospitals with an average length-of-stay of 30 days or less, while other hospitals are classified as long-term hospitals with an average length-of-stay of 30 days or more. The short term hospitals focus their care on acute medical and surgical problems which are anticipated to be resolved in thirty or less days; the long term hospitals focus their care on chronic medical/surgical problems which are anticipated to be resolved in thirty or more days.

About 90% of hospitals in the United States are classified as short-term hospitals. The average length-of-stay for all patients in short-term hospitals in 1990 was 7.2 days and has been decreasing since then. For the older reader it is difficult to imagine that the average length-of-stay for a normal delivery of a baby with no complications is now 2 days or less; or 4 days or less for pneumonia with no complications in someone 17 years of age or younger; or 2 days or less for the repair of an inguinal hernia with no complications; or 7 days for a myocardial infarction (coronary occlusion) without complications. However, studies have shown that there are wide variations geographically on the average length-of-stay in a hospital for patients with the same diagnosis and demographic characteristics. These studies have suggested that these variations are not random variations.

Another way of distinguishing one hospital from another is by their categorization as a <u>general hospital</u> or <u>special hospital</u>. These designations are made according to the type of services offered by the hospital. For the general hospital, the minimum of services offered are medical and surgical. Most general hospitals, however, offer and provide a much wider range of services including medical, surgical, obstetric, pediatric, psychiatric and emergency services. Additionally, many general hospitals also offer supporting services such as social work, psychological, physical therapy, occupational, speech and rehabilitative services. Some of these general hospitals (according to the JCAHO listing) can offer up to 40 different kinds of services. Most hospitals in the United States are general hospitals. The other category of hospitals is that of a special hospital which offers services for select diseases (e.g.. chest disease, cancer, heart disease) or for select populations (e.g., children, rehabilitation patients). By comparison to the general hospital the number of special hospitals is small. The value, however, of such special hospitals is great because of the specialized staff, services and equipment they have available to meet the needs of the select population.

A third means of categorizing hospitals is by the type of <u>hospital ownership</u>. There are three types of ownership: a <u>private not-for-profit owner</u>; a <u>private for-profit owner</u>; and a <u>public owner</u>, (the federal, state, county/city government). The owners of a hospital set the policy (ground rules) which governs and guides the type and operation of a hospital. The designation of a hospital as privately owned is to differentiate it from the publicly owned hospital. Privately owned hospitals, whether for-profit or not-for-profit, are also known as community hospitals because they are available to serve the community at large. This is distinct from the publicly owned hospitals of the federal government which serve select populations such as the Veteran's Hospitals, the Armed Services Hospitals. Though county and city hospitals are public hospitals, they are also community hospitals (serving the public at large). A private not-for-profit hospital is also referred to as a voluntary hospital, referring to its ownership by a voluntary organization, as distinct from a private for-profit hospital which is referred to as a proprietary hospital because of its ownership by a proprietor(s).

The majority of hospitals in the United States are <u>private not-for-profit</u> hospitals, comprising 55% of all hospitals in comparison to the 31% of all hospitals which are publicly owned and the 14% of investor-owned hospitals. The trend at the present time is for an increase in the number of <u>for-profit</u> (investor owned) hospitals. Many private <u>not-for-profit</u> hospitals are under serious fire in regard to their tax-exempt status and benefits because of the changes which many of these hospitals have undergone in order to become more business oriented, namely, to maximize income while lowering expenses, to enter the market place as entrepreneurs, and to meet the competition of other hospitals.

The earlier historical model for the <u>private for-profit hospital</u> in the United States was that of a physician or physicians (residing and practicing in a given community) who invested their own funds to become the proprietor(s) of a hospital for the purpose of providing the services of a hospital but for a profit. The current model for a private for-profit hospital is basically similar to the earlier model, namely, a group of individual investors (not necessarily physicians) who form a corporation and invest the funds of the corporation in owning a hospital, setting the policy for the hospital, and securing a profit for the investors. Because of the profit motive, these hospitals are not tax exempt and therefore are not granted the tax benefits of the not for profit hospital.

It has been during the past decade more than in any prior period of time that the greatest spurt for development of private-for-profit hospitals has taken place as it became evident to investors that hospitals and health care could be Big Business. Most of these private for-profit hospitals are owned by large corporations, with their stock traded on Wall Street, and with their funds able to buy, merge, and acquire hard-pressed private not-for-profit hospitals, as well as construct and operate new hospitals. It should be noted that during the "heyday" of the growth of these private-for-profit hospitals, it was postulated that these more business-oriented hospitals would be more efficient and a less costly service than the not-for-profit hospitals, while maintaining quality of services and assuring continued service to the medically indigent. Recent studies have not totally confirmed these postulates. It has been shown that, in keeping with the need to assure profits to their investors, the private for-profit hospitals may be attracting the more profitable patient (younger, healthier, less sick, more able to self pay or pay from insurance, and more apt to respond more quickly to treatment) while leaving the less profitable patient (older, sicker, chronic medical and surgical problems, less able to pay) to the private not-for-profit hospitals.

In the third type of hospital ownership, the government (federal, state, county, city) is the owner. This type is designated as a <u>public hospital</u>. Thus the government, as the owner, sets the policy, oversees the operation of the hospital and utilizes public funds for the construction and operation of the hospital. Hospitals which are federally or state owned are not viewed as community hospitals because they serve a special population such as the military or veterans or the mentally ill or the mentally retarded or criminally insane. Distinct from these federal or state hospitals, city and county hospitals are very similar to private not-for-profit community general hospitals, except that these hospitals, as public hospitals, are always available to the medically indigent. In the evolution of our hospitals in the United States, it was the city and county hospitals which always were the last port of call to all who required hospitalization regardless of economic means. In this regard, under the current financial pressure which many hospitals are experiencing, the patients who are being under served and "turned" away by these private not-for-profit and for-profit community hospitals are being referred to and accepted at our city/county hospitals. Almost a return to the "last port of call" role of the earlier public hospitals.

There are several additional ways by which hospitals can be categorized, namely, a hospital which offers a primary or secondary or tertiary level of care, a teaching or non-teaching hospital, a hospital which is part of a medical center/ an academic medical center/an academic health center, and finally, a hospital which is part of a multi-hospital system. The level of care categorization is very similar to the categorization of medical care which had been utilized by the armed services, namely, the front line field (primary) hospital, the secondary hospital utilized to back up several field hospitals, and then the large tertiary care hospital backing up the secondary hospitals. The smaller community hospital (almost serving as a neighborhood hospital) can provide the "front line" primary care level for patients with short-term, acute and uncomplicated medical and surgical problems not requiring intensive and extensive specialized diagnosis and treatment. The larger community hospital, in the form of the acute general short-term hospital, can offer both primary and secondary level of care for both uncomplicated and complicated medical, surgical, obstetric, and pediatric problems. At the other end of the spectrum are the teaching hospitals which can offer primary and secondary level of care but also can serve as a tertiary level of care hospital "back stopping" the primary and secondary hospitals in the region with their highly trained and specialized experts, their high technology and equipment and staff required for the diagnosis, treatment, and management of the serious and complicated medical, surgical and other problems, such as, open-heart surgery, organ transplants, newer anti-cancer medication, high-risk patients. In the current scene of cost containment, tertiary care academic medical centers may also serve as "Centers of Excellence" (described elsewhere).

Skeletons in the Medical Closet
A Personal Story and a Professional Report

Although many hospitals are involved in the education of physicians, nurses and the other health professions, a teaching hospital is a designation usually given to a hospital which is formally (contractually) affiliated with a medical school or a hospital which is owned and operated by a university/medical school. These teaching hospitals have been for the most part private not-for-profit hospitals or public hospitals. More recently some teaching hospitals have been acquired by for profit corporations. The university-owned and operated hospitals are known as academic medical centers (consisting of a hospital or hospitals and the medical school) or as an academic health center (consisting of a hospital or hospitals, a medical school, a nursing school, a pharmacy school, a dental school, a health-related school for physical/occupational therapists, medical record specialists, clinical laboratory technicians).

A teaching hospital is a hospital which focuses its resources (staff, physical plant, funds) on clinical services, clinical teaching and clinical research. A teaching hospital utilizes its patients for the education and training of the medical/nursing/dental/health-related students, the interns, residents and fellows of the various specialties of medicine. A tax exempt teaching hospital solicits and secures federal and foundation funds for conduct of research and may utilize selected and consenting patients for clinical research. Though teaching hospitals in the United States comprise only 6% of all hospitals, they have 20% of all hospital beds, command 30% of the total payroll of all hospitals, spend 28% of all expenditures, employ 50% of all full-time physicians in hospitals, and have 70% of all the interns and residents. As can be seen and surmised, the teaching hospital is a very significant and important component in the network of hospitals in the United States. This significance is reflected for examples: in the fact that Medicare and other third-party payors provide an increased level of reimbursement for patient care to teaching hospitals. as compared with non-teaching hospitals; in the fact that all of the "best hospitals" listed in the surveys of such nature are teaching hospitals (Best of Medicine, U.S. News & World Report 1990).

Finally, the newest type of classification for a hospital is that of a hospital which is part of a <u>multi-hospital system</u>. This category has emerged during the past two to three decades, as there were no multi-hospital systems in 1960. In 1987 there were 2,400 multiple hospital systems; in 1990 there 2,862 such systems; and in 1995 it was expected that there would be 3,400 such systems. The multi-hospital system can include private-for-profit hospitals and private not-for-profit hospitals. In 1987, 26 private for profit organizations owned 967 of these multi-hospital systems, while 138 private not-for-profit systems owned 1,064 hospitals. By 1997 the number of investor owned multi-hospital systems had doubled or tripled. A multi-hospital system emerges when several hospitals agree to merge and consolidate their organizations, services and staff in order to take economic advantage of the centralized purchasing, maintenance, billing and record keeping while also concentrating different services in each of the hospitals. In this way a multi-hospital system is a system corporation which owns, leases and manages two or more hospitals and health and health-related facilities, such as an acute short-term general hospital, a long-term hospital for chronic disease, a nursing home, a smaller community hospital, a home health care center, an urgent care center, a clinical laboratory. It should be noted that in a most recent survey by a major health consulting company, the multi-hospital system was deemed to be the "wave of the future" in hospital development.

Though it is difficult to specifically describe the advantages of one category of hospital over another because of the wide range of patient likes and dislikes and the wide range of hospital types, it is possible to describe these differences in general terms.

To begin with, most of the short-term, general community hospitals, whether private for-profit or not-for-profit, can offer clinical services and patient care which is responsive to most acute, uncomplicated and less serious medical and surgical problems. It is possible that the for profit hospitals can offer more creature comforts because of available capital money, and more effective marketing and purchasing, but they may also provide easier access for patients with less complicated problems and a greater financial ability to pay (better insurance policies). As noted elsewhere the special hospitals, and especially for children, can offer their special population staff, equipment and services which are more specialized, in keeping with the unique needs of the select population served. Some long-term hospitals (60 days or more) may be much more geared to the patient whose illness is a chronic one requiring less active and vigorous management but requiring longer term care and for this reason will have a smaller staff-per-patient ratio because of less need for extensive and intensive services (235 full-time employees/100 patients as compared with 534/100 patients for a short-term hospital). The smaller community hospital may offer a more comfortable and neighborly environment for patient care but may have less full-time physicians or residents/interns available at all times than the larger community hospitals. The teaching hospital, academic medical center or academic health center tends to be a large noisy, bustling, impersonal hospital with a large number of full-time physicians and health-related professionals available at all times, as well as a large house staff of "learners" for each patient, and for this reason can provide the most advanced and professional and technical expertise, as well as the latest equipment and knowledge for the diagnosis and treatment of the more and most serious complicated medical and surgical problems.

How A Hospital Works: General Comments

The modern hospital of today is a labor-intensive business relying on its 200 different categories of employees to carry out its mission. In some communities the hospital is the area's largest employer and purchaser of food and other products. The

Meyer Sonis M.D.

hospital, whether a small 100 bed hospital or a large 1000 bed teaching hospital, is open for business every day and night of the year regardless of whether its beds are fully or partly occupied. Not only must the hospital serve as a hotel, with all of the responsibilities of such, but it must also serve as a medical mall for sick people with the objective of providing safe, competent and quality care for their medical and surgical problems. With so many hands conducting so many activities at so many different times, it is easy to understand why failures in and of hospitals might and do occur. The ways and means through which a hospital achieves its objectives and harnesses so many hands will be described in the remainder of this chapter.

Though hospitals do differ one from another, they all generally conduct their business along similar lines: the designation of a group of people as the ultimate persons responsible and accountable for all of the activities of the hospital; the promulgation by this authority of the ground rules for conduct of hospital business; the utilization of an organizational structure of authority and accountability through which the hospital can support its staff, services and programs; the employment by the hospital of the personnel required to deliver its services and programs; the maintenance of educational/training/clinical experience criteria by the hospital so that the competence and skill of its personnel is assured; the utilization by the hospital of methods and personnel to monitor and evaluate the performance of the staff and the safety, competence and quality of services which are rendered; and finally, the maintenance of finances required for the hospital to achieve its objectives.

Skeletons in the Medical Closet
A Personal Story and a Professional Report

How A Hospital Works: Its Owners

Before a hospital can receive its first patient, whether such a hospital was founded 50 years ago or today, it must be established in the eyes of the law (federal, state and local governments) as a legal entity. This enables the government(s) to know who will own and operate this business (hospital), who will be fiscally and legally accountable for all activities in which the hospital will engage and what are the purposes of the hospital. By establishing itself as a legal entity, in keeping with the rules and regulations laid down for hospitals by the government(s), the hospital will be in a position to: be granted its status as a tax exempt or non tax exempt hospital; receive, spend and account for monies utilized, as a for-profit or not-for-profit business; conduct the legal purposes of the hospital; secure the various licenses required and meet the nationally accepted standards established for operation as a hospital; employ the personnel and develop the physical plant required to pursue the wide range of activities required. This initial step, of establishing the hospital as a legal entity, is usually taken by a group of persons who are interested in the hospital as a service to the community or as an investment of their money. This group of persons, known as the Board of Directors or Board of Trustees, submits all information required by the governments, such as of articles of incorporation, bylaws, financial statements. Once the hospital is a legal entity this Board of Directors serves as the recognized and accountable authority for all activities of the hospital.

This Board of Directors serves as the owner, landlord and government of the hospital. It is this Board of Directors which is held legally and fiscally accountable for all actions of the hospital, whether good or bad, whether performed by a physician or others, and whether performed in the patient's room or operating room. As the government of the hospital, the Board of Directors promulgates and monitors the implementation of the rules and regulations which will govern and serve as guidelines for all activities of the hospital, ranging from personnel practices for employees, to what services and programs can be offered, to the appointment of the physicians who can attend patients in the hospital, to monitoring the performance of staff, and to the quality of services provided. Unfortunately this point of promulgating, maintaining, and monitoring of all programs is often forgotten by the members of a Board of Directors of a hospital. This was brought home most recently in a notorious situation in the Commonwealth of Pennsylvania and which has been reported in the national news. Parenthetically, it is the same hospital referred to by me in my personal story about my wife's death. In the notorious situation referred to, a bankruptcy court has held the Board of Directors of this hospital accountable for the almost 2 billion dollar debacle which had been produced on their watch by "shoddy" practices and fiscal irregularities in their acquisition of medical schools and other hospitals.

It should be noted that, because of the complexities of a modern hospital in its wide range of services, programs, personnel, patients, the Board of Directors of our modern hospitals require a great deal more in activities of their members than was the case in the hospitals of the past. The possible scope of activities in a hospital over which a Board of Directors governs and functions, can be gleaned from: the wide array of clinical services which a hospital can offer, such as alcohol/drug dependence programs, diagnostic and therapeutic radiology, emergency, dietetic, medical and surgical services, special care units (coronary care, burn, renal, transplant, intensive), oncology, and psychiatry, but to mention a few of the more than sixty possible different services; the wide array of standards established by accreditation and licensing authorities for plant safety, fire prevention, control of hospital infections, blood transfusions, tissue pathology examination, medical records, patient care, monitoring, mortality reports, credentials of physicians, and which must be adhered to by the hospital; the wide array of third party payors; the broad scope of patients served but to mention a few of these activities requiring oversight by a Board of Directors.

In order for a Board of Directors of a hospital to maintain its vigilance over the range of functions and responsibilities for which they are accountable various procedures and mechanisms are utilized by them. Among these mechanisms are: regularly scheduled meetings of the Board of Directors held throughout the year; the utilization of various Committees of the Board of Directors (consisting of various members of the Board of Directors), who meet more frequently than the entire Board and provide periodic reports to the Board (i.e., executive committee, finance committee, personnel committee, quality control committee, infection control committee, medical liaison committee, etc.); a weekly or biweekly meeting between the Executive Committee of the Board and the Chief Executive Officer (manager/ administrator) of the hospital; monthly reports of the chief executive officer to the Board of Directors; periodic reports to the Board of Directors by key administrative and professional staff; and periodic audits and audit reports of the hospital's finances.

In a non-profit hospital the members of the Board of Directors are not employees of the hospital. Rather they are influential civic and industrial leaders, prominent citizens of the community, philanthropic persons who have volunteered their time, energy and at times their own funds in order to serve the community good. As our modern hospital has evolved into the complex organization required to keep pace with the competitive health care market, and as our society has become a more "open" one, membership on the Board of Directors of a not-for-profit hospital has changed so as to also include attorneys, accountants, public relations specialists, representatives of labor, consumer and minority groups. Because of potential conflicts of interest, governing bodies of these voluntary hospitals tend to limit the number of physicians who are members of the Board. Smaller communities, and in rural/suburban communities, the members of the Board of Directors of a not-for-profit hospital may cut across the leading citizens of the area. For some hospitals which are not-for-profit teaching hospitals, their Boards of Directors may also include representatives or officers of a university or medical center.

Because a non-profit hospital is a tax exempt institution it is obligated to provide information about their hospital if requested by the public. In keeping with the rights of patients, they can request information from the non-profit hospital about their Board of Directors (names, committees), constitution and by-laws of the hospital, the physician staff, annual report, fiscal report, and their accreditation status.

How A Hospital Works: Its Management

During the hospitalization of a patient there are innumerable employees of the hospital who are involved with the sum total of patient care. Some of these persons and their activities are directly seen and experienced by the patient, since these persons and activities are concerned with the <u>clinical care rendered</u> a patient (the diagnosis and treatment of the medical or surgical problems of the patient) and with the <u>human care</u> provided a patient (lodging, food, housekeeping, telephone, visitor comfort, etc.). Others of these persons and activities are seldom, if ever, directly seen or experienced by the patient, since these persons and activities are concerned with the <u>business care and standards of patient care</u> (typing, purchasing, cashier, finances, personnel practices, quality assurance programs, risk management programs).

It is, therefore, the task of the hospital management to bring these persons and activities together on behalf of the patient in as effective, timely, appropriate and coordinated a manner as possible, while holding those persons performing the activities responsible and accountable for the results and outcome of

Skeletons in the Medical Closet
A Personal Story and a Professional Report

patient care. Apropos of this task facing the management of a hospital, recent studies (referred to in a previous chapter) of the failures in and of hospitals have suggested that a major reason for such system failures in a hospital is the lack of and/or breakdown in communication and coordination between the various personnel who carry out patient activities.

For most modern hospitals in the United States, hospital management is guided by the principles of organization and operation which are similar (only varying by degree) from one hospital to the other depending on size, type and purpose of the hospital. These principles generally follow this pattern. The Board of Directors serve as the owners, landlord and government of the hospital and are the ultimate and final authority for all activities and personnel of the hospital. As the final authority the Board of Directors employs (hires and fires) the primary person who will serve as the Chief Executive Officer (administrator/manager) of the hospital, and who will be directly and totally responsible and accountable to the Board of Directors for carrying out the policy established by the Board. The Board of Directors and Chief Executive Officer will then establish, in pyramid fashion, a direct chain of command (channels of communication, coordination, supervision, accountability from the Chief Executive Officer down) for all personnel and activities of the hospitals. The chain of command will centralize accountability for all personnel and activities of the hospital in the hands of a few persons at the top of the pyramid who will report to the Chief Executive Officer while decentralizing responsibility for the direct performance of activities to the individual persons at the bottom of the pyramid. The physicians of the hospital, as will be detailed in a later section of this chapter, will assume total responsibility for all decisions about the medical and surgical care of the patient but will be held accountable to carry out these decisions within the guidelines established by the hospital. Finally, all personnel with similar functions, education and credentials carrying out similar activities will be grouped into distinct units/programs/divisions/departments.

For purposes of illustration, attention is called to the following pictorial representation on page 133 of a "sample" hospital organization. Hospitals may differ from this sample by degree, depending on size, type and purpose. As can be surmised, a hospital is very much like any business enterprise, with the smallest number of people serving as executive personnel, a larger number of people serving as senior and junior level managers, and the largest number of employees serving as production workers. For most hospitals, the staff (employees) consists of a professional and technical group of personnel spread out between the medical staff, professional and nursing services offering clinical care as distinct from the administrative, managerial and support personnel offering human, business and standards of care. Since it can impact on the care patients receive, and as with other enterprises, there are pecking orders, turf issues, and status and prestige problems between the different classes of personnel of the hospital. In the past evolution of our modern hospital, and perhaps still continuing to a lesser degree now, hospitals were notorious for the non-competitive nature of their salary and benefits plans for non-physician employees, as compared with similar employees in other enterprises. Therefore, it is comparatively easy to understand the feelings of anger, envy and dissatisfaction which can be generated in different classes of hospital personnel by the different classes of status and prestige. It is to the credit of hospitals and their personnel, despite internal issues and problems, that most patients are able to receive successful patient care.

Skeletons in the Medical Closet
A Personal Story and a Professional Report

Model of Hospital Organization Chart

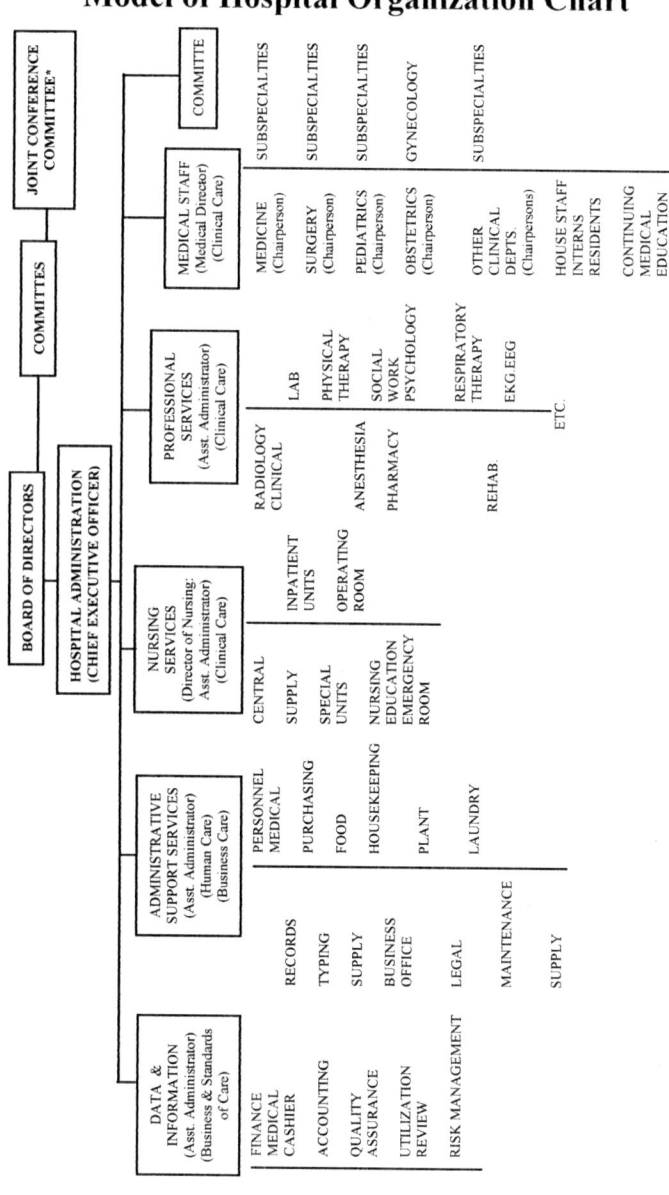

BOARD OF DIRECTORS — COMMITTEES — JOINT CONFERENCE COMMITTEE*

HOSPITAL ADMINISTRATION (CHIEF EXECUTIVE OFFICER)

DATA & INFORMATION (Asst. Administrator) (Business & Standards of Care)
- FINANCE
- MEDICAL CASHIER
- ACCOUNTING
- QUALITY ASSURANCE
- UTILIZATION REVIEW
- RISK MANAGEMENT

ADMINISTRATIVE SUPPORT SERVICES (Asst. Administrator) (Human Care) (Business Care)
- PERSONNEL MEDICAL — RECORDS
- PURCHASING — TYPING
- FOOD — SUPPLY
- HOUSEKEEPING — BUSINESS OFFICE
- PLANT — LEGAL
- LAUNDRY — MAINTENANCE
- SUPPLY

NURSING SERVICES (Director of Nursing: Asst. Administrator) (Clinical Care)
- CENTRAL SUPPLY
- SPECIAL UNITS
- NURSING EDUCATION
- EMERGENCY ROOM
- INPATIENT UNITS
- OPERATING ROOM

PROFESSIONAL SERVICES (Asst. Administrator) (Clinical Care)
- RADIOLOGY CLINICAL
- ANESTHESIA
- PHARMACY
- REHAB
- LAB
- PHYSICAL THERAPY
- SOCIAL WORK
- PSYCHOLOGY
- RESPIRATORY THERAPY
- EKG EEG
- ETC.

MEDICAL STAFF (Medical Director) (Clinical Care) — COMMITTEE
- MEDICINE (Chairperson) — SUBSPECIALTIES
- SURGERY (Chairperson) — SUBSPECIALTIES
- PEDIATRICS (Chairperson) — SUBSPECIALTIES
- OBSTETRICS (Chairperson) — GYNECOLOGY
- OTHER CLINICAL DEPTS. (Chairpersons) — SUBSPECIALTIES
- HOUSE STAFF INTERNS RESIDENTS
- CONTINUING MEDICAL EDUCATION

*Joint Conference Committee: representatives from Board of Directors and Medical Staff

Meyer Sonis M.D.

For most hospitals, the Chief Executive Officer is not a physician but a person with specialized graduate education as a hospital administrator. For the smaller hospitals, the Chief Executive Officer may be an administrator who has a nursing degree or may have advanced from within the hospital ranks. In the past physicians sometimes served as hospital administrators and medical directors. As hospitals became more complex physicians began to primarily serve as medical directors only.

How The Hospital Works: Its Physicians/Its Medical Staff

The physicians who admit, attend and care for the hospitalized patient are the lifeblood of a hospital in more ways than one. To begin with the physician is the only person in the hospital who by law is entitled to practice medicine, i.e., recipient of a medical license. Secondly, since 75% of all admissions of patients to hospitals are on the basis of referral by a physician, the physician is important to the business side of the hospital. For example, if one physician's practice has 100 patients, approximately 20 of them may require hospitalization during the course of a year, utilizing an average of 144 patient days at an average cost of $500/day or an average of $70,000/year in hospital income. This latter point was brought into sharp focus in a recent study which reported that one large group practice of physicians controlled the potential of 20,000 patient hospital days annually from their combined practices and thus controlled a potential annual income to a hospital of $10 million, and for this reason this group of doctors was able to "shop" around for which hospital in their community would give them a "better deal."

For these reasons the physician, within the hospital setting, has a special role and place. Within the hospital the physician "calls all of the shots" about the clinical care of the patient and can act as an independent agent in making and acting on his/her clinical judgments about the patient. At the same time, however, the physician must abide by the rules and regulations promulgated by the hospital and which govern the practice of medicine within the hospital (see later comment about Medical Staff and Medical Staff Bylaws of the Hospital). Because of the importance of physicians to hospitals, physicians are given special consideration in their relationship to the authority of the Board of Directors via a formal organizational structure from the Medical Staff to the Board of Directors through a Joint Conference Committee, so that physicians can have a direct voice in the setting of policy (ground rules) by the Board of Directors. Within the hospital setting the physician is at the top of the pecking order, but with some physicians able to peck harder. It is because of this duality in the role and place of the physician within the hospital setting, namely on the one hand able to be independent of the hospital authority in making clinical decisions but on the other hand being dependent on the hospital for admitting privileges, that problems and challenges for physicians (from time immemorial) have been posed for the management of a hospital in the task of harnessing, monitoring and coordinating physician activities. Apropos of these problems and challenges in the relationship of physicians to the hospital it has been suggested that, because hospitals and physicians will both be under severe economic pressure in the next decade, there will be much greater integration between a hospital and its physicians so that a new kind of hospital-physician organizational structure will evolve to give more power to the physician in a hospital than currently is the case but also will bind the physician more exclusively to the hospital.

In the evolution of our predecessor hospital to the modern hospital of today significant changes have taken place in the role, responsibility and place of a physician within a hospital setting. In the past, for many of our smaller community hospitals, the physicians who admitted and attended their patients in the hospital were comparatively independent agents with few restrictions or monitoring of their performances. He or she could practice a specialty in the hospital as a self-designated physician specialist without specialized education or training except for his/her experience. The medical staff organization of the hospital did not have much authority over this independent physician. As the national standards governing accreditation of hospitals became more stringent, and as physician practice in a hospital became more complex and specialized, the medical staff organization of a hospital became more structured and meaningful so that the physician of the past became more "domesticated" within a hospital setting, namely, the establishment of rules, regulations, guidelines to govern all physicians practicing within the hospital setting but with sanctions on the physician if infractions occur.

In the United States, the standards which govern clinical practice within a modern hospital of today have been established by the various accreditation authorities. In keeping with these standards, the hospital must group all physicians who are entitled to practice medicine within that hospital into a single formal body, called the Medical Staff of the hospital. This Medical Staff "has overall responsibility for the quality of professional services provided by individuals with clinical privileges, as well as responsibility for accounting therefore to the governing body." These standards call for the development and approval by the Medical Staff of the hospital of a formal framework called Medical Staff Bylaws, for the "self-governance of medical staff activity and accountability." This formal document, which in turn must be approved by the Board of Directors of the hospital, provides the rules, regulations and sanctions which govern the organization and operation of the Medical Staff. It is to be kept in mind that, as with the By-Laws of a nonprofit hospital, the Medical Staff By-Laws are available to the public on request.

The significance of the medical staff by-laws, for the physician and for the physician's hospitalized patient, can be seen in the wide scope and range of physician-patient activities which are covered. For examples, the medical staff by-laws provide rules and regulations covering: the criteria for becoming an attending physician at the hospital in order to admit and attend patients; the ways and means whereby a physician can make application and be appointed to the Medical Staff; the nature and extent of the clinical privileges (patient procedures) which that physician may be given to practice within the hospital, depending on his or her credentials (education, training, experience, references); the various ways and means for monitoring and evaluating the performance of individual physician members in the clinical care provided by them to their patients (i.e., quality assurance programs and peer review committees); and the sanctions to be imposed if a member of the medical staff does not abide by the rules and regulations of the medical staff bylaws. Currently and probably even more in the future, under the pressures of consumer and third party payors of hospital services, increasing emphasis is being and will be given by the medical staffs of hospitals to monitoring: the credentials of a physician member, as the basis for delineating the limits of his or her practice within the hospital to perform procedures, to conduct studies; the performance record of physician members in their medical or surgical care such as their patient death rate, adverse events, infections; the safety, competence and quality of care provided by each physician to his/her patient, as seen through the quality improvement programs of the hospital and medical staff.

Depending on its size, type, purpose, and range of services offered, one hospital may vary from another hospital in the internal organization of their Medical Staff. Generally, however, the Medical Staff conducts its business through: scheduled periodic meetings of the entire Medical Staff; the officers who are elected by the Medical Staff members, and who serve as the executive committee for business conducted between the regular meetings of the Medical Staff; the various committees and their formal reports. Officers, committee members, and members of the Medical Staff serve with no fee or compensation for their services on the Medical Staff. Among the major committees of the Medical Staff, which are vital to the care of the hospitalized patient, are those of the Credential Committee, the Medical Records Committee, the Tissue Committee, the Medical Audit Committee (all of which will be described subsequently under The Doctor and Hospital Watchers), and the Joint Conference Committee which serves as the link between the activities of the Medical Staff and its members and the Board of Directors of the hospital. Within the guidelines established and monitored by the Medical Staff of a hospital, the physician generalists and specialists admit their own patients, prescribe and order tests for their patients, follow the patient during the course of hospitalization, call in consultants as needed, and decide on the patient's discharge. However, the admission, hospital course and discharge of patients by a physician are also currently stringently scrutinized by the different Medical Staff Committees and by third party payors.

As the field of medicine changed into the more complex and specialized practice of medicine, as the various specialties and subspecialties in medicine and surgery emerged with their specialized certification regulations, as the larger hospitals emerged with their increased capacity to offer a wide range of services, as the medical schools and their teaching hospitals became a significant force in the health service industry, and as the standard setting bodies and third party payors began to have more influence, the previous role of the physician as a comparatively independent agent within the hospital began to shift. Under these changing circumstances the rules and regulations of the medical staff organization of a hospital became more meaningful: hospitals increasingly employed full time medical directors to "oversee" the operation of the medical staff; the place of the independent physician shifted to that of a full time salaried employee; the physicians in the hospital become more "domesticated and integrated" with the administration and management of the hospital. Along with this

Skeletons in the Medical Closet
A Personal Story and a Professional Report

shift, conflict and controversy emerged between the "town" physicians (the private sector practice of medicine) and the increasing number of "gown" and salaried physicians (the full time practice of hospital medicine) regarding the unfair competition of "gown" physicians because of their "guaranteed salary and benefit plans," (retirement, vacation, malpractice insurance, disability coverage, etc.) and perquisites (no office expenses, low cost parking, "company" car, etc.).

In summary, it is only within the structure of the Medical Staff of the hospital (its rules, regulations and method for monitoring the performance of a physician member of that staff) that the activities of a physician in the modern hospital of today can be viewed. First of all, the patient's physician must be a member of the Medical Staff of the hospital in order to admit and discharge the patient. Secondly, the patient's physician must be guided by and abide by the rules, regulations, policy and procedures established by the medical staff for admission, care and discharge. Third, the patient's physician must be responsible for the ongoing clinical care of the patient during hospitalization (direct contact with patient, ordering tests/procedures, securing specialist consultation) but only within the limits of his/her privileges at the hospital. Lastly, the patient's physician must be prepared to have sanctions imposed on him/her for infraction of the established rules.

How A Hospital Works: Its Nurses

Before proceeding with my abbreviated focus on the hospital and its nurses, perhaps a brief word is needed about the nursing profession/nursing industry. In all fairness to the importance of the nursing industry in the medical and human care of all patients, reference is made in the appendix to selected readings. At the present time it is estimated that about two to three million persons are licensed in the United States to practice in the field of nursing. All of these nurses have completed their requirements to practice as an R.N. (Registered Nurse), namely, they have successfully passed the licensure examination in their state. Nurses who comprise the nursing industry include the following categories: <u>Nurse's Aide</u>, who is a high school graduate or its equivalent plus a period of supervised training in a hospital; <u>Licensed Practical Nurse</u> (L.P.N.), who is a high school graduate with one year of formal training in a hospital school of nursing, and with a license to practice as L.P.N.; <u>Diploma Nurse</u>, who is a high school graduate with two to three years of formal education and training in a hospital school of nursing, in addition to a license as R.N; <u>Associate Degree Nurse</u> (A.N.), who is a high school graduate with two years of formal education in a community college, affiliated with a hospital school of nursing plus holding a license as R.N.; <u>Baccalaureate Degree Nurse</u> (B.S. in Nursing), who is a high school graduate with four years of formal education and training in a school of nursing of a university, plus license as R.N.; <u>Master's Degree Nurse</u> (M.A. or M.Sc. in Nursing), who is a college graduate with two formal years of education in a post graduate nursing education program of a university plus license as R.N., <u>Doctorate Degree in Nursing</u> (Ph.D. in Nursing or D.N.), who has a Master's Degree in Nursing, with two to three years in a post graduate doctorate nursing education program of a school of nursing in a University, plus license as R.N.; <u>Nurse Clinician or Nurse Practitioner</u>, who usually has a Master's Degree in Nursing from a university school of nursing plus two years of specialized training in a hospital, plus license as R.N. Exclusive of the LPN and Nursing Aide category, it is estimated (1995) that 57% of R.N.'s have diploma/associate degrees in nursing, 34% of R.N.'s have a Baccalaureate Degree in Nursing. and 9% of R.N.'s have advanced degrees in nursing.. It is also estimated that of all R.N.'s almost 70% are employed by hospitals while the other 30% are distributed among physician's offices, nursing homes, public health offices, and nursing education programs.

Skeletons in the Medical Closet
A Personal Story and a Professional Report

Up until 1970 most of the R.N.'s in the country received their education and training in the School of Nursing of a community hospital. As a consequence of the significant scientific advances in medicine and surgery since 1970, a shift occurred in the preparation for becoming a nurse towards more formal education and training. These standards for the education and training of nurses were initially established, periodically revised and continuously monitored by national accreditation bodies, such as the American Nurse's Association, National League for Nursing, Association of College School's of Nursing, Joint Commission of Accreditation of Health Organizations, State Boards of Nursing Licensure.

Of all the personnel in a hospital with whom the patient will have contact during hospitalization, it is the nursing service and its staff with whom the patient will have the most and continuous contact. These contacts can range from the initial history taking (in order to draw up a nursing plan for the patient), to the provision of the bed pan, to the medication given during the three shifts, to the monitoring of vital signs (pulse, temperature, respirations) following surgery, to the help needed to eat, to the discharge discussion prior to the patient leaving. In light of this extensive contact with patients almost half of all hospital employees are members of the nursing service. Though hospitals may differ from each other in the specifics of their nursing services, the comments to follow are generally applicable to all hospitals.The nursing service of most of our modern hospitals is usually established as a distinct administrative and programmatic component of the total organizational structure of the hospital (see pictorial organization of a hospital). The personnel of the hospital usually assigned to the nursing service will include the total range of registered nurses, licensed practical nurses, nurses' aides/orderlies/ attendants. As noted previously the standards for the nursing service of a hospital have been developed and monitored by the national accreditation authorities.

Meyer Sonis M.D.

In keeping with these standards, the nursing service of a hospital is usually under the direction of a qualified registered nurse who serves as the director of the nursing service, and who may also serve as an assistant administrator of the hospital with responsibility and accountability to the administrator/chief executive officer for all activities of the nursing service. In pyramid style, the Nursing Service is organized in a centralized fashion for purposes of assignment, coordination, scheduling, supervision, monitoring and evaluation of all nursing personnel and their activities, and in a decentralized fashion for the purpose of day to day implementation of duties assigned to nursing personnel at their geographic location in the hospital (for examples, direct patient care in the hospital room, operating room or special care unit.

During these past 50 years the pattern and practice of nursing care within a hospital has undergone major transitions. At one time (1930-1950) the model of nursing care in a hospital was that of one nurse assigned to provide all nursing functions to several patients during one shift. As the clinical care of a patient became more complex, coupled with the development of a nursing shortage, the model of bedside nursing care changed several times from that of the earlier model of care. At first to a model of care wherein clerks were utilized to maintain records, aides were assigned to maintenance and bed care duties, one nurse assigned responsibility for securing and distributing medication to all patients, and one nurse was assigned responsibility for treatment activities. Then the model of nursing care shifted, wherein a "team" of personnel of the Nursing Service would cover all nursing functions for a group of patients, with the less trained personnel supervised by the more trained and with all monitored by a team leader during one shift. This model was followed by a partial return to the earlier model of the 1930-1950's, wherein (a primary care model) one nurse on each shift would assume responsibility and accountability for overseeing, managing, coordinating, planning all clinical and

Skeletons in the Medical Closet
A Personal Story and a Professional Report

human care services provided to a small number of patients and then on to the most recent model of nursing care practice, namely, the <u>case manager nursing model of practice</u>, wherein one nurse assumes responsibility for development and implementation of the nursing care plan for those patients assigned, including overseeing and managing all other non-physician personnel providing clinical care to the patient during the total hospitalization of the patient. With these various changes in nursing practice, as well as changes in the profession of nursing, have also emerged a changing role for the nurse within the hospital setting. This new role recognized the basic clinical knowledge and skill of the qualified nurse so that a nurse could assume greater responsibility to complement and supplement the physician in the care of the hospitalized patient and in the monitoring of the quality patient care. Thus, within the current hospital setting, the qualified nurse has assumed greater and greater responsibility for: the specialized care required in the special units of the hospital, such as the intensive care unit, coronary care unit, transplantation unit, burn unit, renal dialysis unit, trauma unit; performance and direction of activities relative to monitoring the standards of care; serving as a nurse clinical specialist or practitioner for selected populations, i. e., psychiatric, pediatric, midwife. In keeping with these increased responsibilities qualified nurses have become nurse anesthetists, nurse phlebotomists (venipuncture), directors of utilization review/ quality assurance and risk management programs of hospitals.

How a Hospital Works: Other Professional Services

In order to diagnose and treat the various medical and surgical problems of the hospitalized patient, the attending physician often times will require the aid of other professional services. These other professional services are not routinely provided to all hospitalized patients (as is room and board), but are selectively

Meyer Sonis M.D.

provided only at the request/order of the attending physician/physician in charge of a patient's care. Among these many other professional services which can be brought into play by the attending physician are those of the clinical laboratory (pathology and medical laboratory), radiology (x-ray), anesthesiology, pharmacy, physical therapy, rehabilitation (psychological, social work, others), recreational therapy, speech/language and audiology, respiratory care, electro-cardiograph and other cardiac tests, electroencephalograph (sleep studies). With the continued advances in medical technology, newer categories of other professional services are continually being added to this list. These services, when they are provided, are charged to the hospitalized patient as a separate cost item from that of room and board. It must be noted that some of these other professional services have become high volume and income generating services for the hospital, such as the clinical laboratory, radiology and anesthesiology services.

With the very significant advances which have been made during the past few decades in our knowledge base about the normal body (its organs, tissues and fluids), the changes which are produced by disease/illness/defects/trauma, and about the diagnosis and treatment of medical and surgical problems, the clinical laboratory, radiology and anesthesia services of a modern hospital have become a far cry from these same services in our predecessor hospital of yesterday. As a consequence, these services have undergone major growth in their size (personnel, equipment) and in their capabilities of providing the modern physician with information needed to assist the physician in his/her diagnosis and treatment of the hospitalized patient. In keeping with the growth of these services, standards have been developed and established by national and local bodies of accreditation and licensing regarding: the basic education, training, supervision and monitoring of the personnel performing such services; the accuracy, effectiveness and safety of equipment utilized; the accuracy of data secured and

Skeletons in the Medical Closet
A Personal Story and a Professional Report

interpreted/analyzed; and the timeliness and appropriateness of all reports and records generated.

The functions of the <u>Clinical Laboratory</u> of a modern hospital are quite varied and complex. It performs hematologic (blood), bacteriological (germs and viruses), biochemical (chemistry) studies on hospitalized patients requiring such. It monitors the collection, distribution, safety of blood and blood products and operates a blood bank. It monitors and operates an organ bank. It conducts microscopic and other studies of tissues removed during surgery and autopsies. It prepares timely and appropriate reports on all studies conducted and participates in all activities of the hospital (i.e., committees) which require the expertise available within a department of pathology/medical laboratory. Depending on the size and complexity of the hospital, some of their clinical laboratories are able to perform studies of the most routine nature to those of a more esoteric nature, while others may contract with an independent laboratory to perform complicated studies.

The <u>Radiology Service</u> of a modern hospital has a wide scope of tools available, as compared to the X-ray Departments of only twenty years ago. These tools include: fluoroscopy (utilizing x-ray beams to view organs against a fluorescent screen); radiography (utilizing x-ray beams to view bodily organs in the form of a still picture on a film); cineradiology (utilizing x-ray beams to view organs in the form of a motion picture on a film); contrast fluoroscopy, radiography, cineradiography (utilizing a dye to film an organ and its functioning); angiography (utilizing a dye to inject into the blood stream in order to visualize an organ and its function); computerized axial tomography (CAT Scans utilizing x-ray beams to rapidly secure a whole series of three dimensional views on film of organs, as if the organ were sliced into thin layers); Nuclear Magnetic Resonance (NMR, utilizing a strong magnetic and radio beam to secure a more detailed and magnified view on film of an organ during a time when the nuclei of the cells of that organ are temporarily influenced by a magnetic field);

Meyer Sonis M.D.

Nuclear Radiology, (utilization of radioactive material for injection/ingestion in order to "tag" certain organs for x-ray viewing); Cyclotron and other high emission x-ray beams (utilizing these beams for irradiation of malignant masses); Positive Emission Tomography Scan (PET, utilization of certain selected radio-isotope material in order to film the function of an organ).

The <u>Anesthesia Service</u> of a modern hospital has literally become a "hospital industry" in itself during the past decade or two, and as an outgrowth of the spurt in the quantity and types of surgery undertaken in our modern community hospitals. To illustrate this point even more clearly, consider the task for anesthesia in keeping a patient "painless but alive" for the seven to ten to twelve hours of organ transplantation or the four to five hours of open heart surgery of a patient on a heart-lung bypass machine or the hours required for lung or brain surgery. In order to fulfill this purpose of rendering a patient insensitive to pain while keeping the patient "alive" the anesthesiologist must be able to assess: the medical condition of the patient prior to receipt of anesthesia, in order to determine the nature of anesthesia required; the advantages and disadvantages of the various anesthetic agents; the level of unconsciousness of the patient from moment to moment during surgery; the status of the patient during recovery. The Anesthesia Service also serves as a clinical service for the diagnosis and treatment of pain of the patient associated with various medical conditions.

In keeping with standards established each of these other professional services must be directed and supervised by a qualified physician specialist, who by education, training, and experience is certified by the appropriate authority as a pathologist, radiologist or anesthesiologist. Because of the unique status of these services in our modern hospital, namely, as potentially high income generators and serving patients selectively, the compensation of those physicians performing these services may be different than for other physicians associated with a hospital. These physicians can be compensated in any of several ways, such as, a salaried employee who also receives a bonus based on a percentage of the gross or net receipts of the service, or on a fee for each service rendered (at an agreed upon rate), or as a private for-profit corporation leased to the hospital. In keeping with standards also established for these services, non-physician personnel who serve as technical staff in the performance of these services must meet the requirements of education, training, and experience for them to serve as medical technicians for the clinical laboratory, radiology technicians for the radiology service, and nurse anesthetists for the anesthesia service of a hospital.

How The Hospital Works: Its Pharmacy

The Pharmacy of a hospital is given the role, under the responsibility of a licensed pharmacist, of manufacturing, purchasing, compounding, distributing all of the medications/ chemical agents which are utilized by the hospital in the diagnosis and treatment of its patients. For the smaller hospital, the pharmacy department may be a very limited one and depend on local pharmacies for the scope of medication needed. For the larger hospitals the pharmacy is able to provide for the total potential gamut of material required, ranging from aspirin to intravenous solutions to contrast media dyes to insulin to injectables. The Pharmacy is also viewed as an income producer for the hospital, since charges for all medications can be billed to the patient (third party payor) directly. The profit on medications may vary from hospital to hospital depending on the policy of the hospital.

In the operation of the hospital pharmacy, the established national standards must be met and must be monitored by the rules and regulations of the Medical Staff of the hospital through a Pharmacy and Therapeutic Committee (physicians of the hospital). The task of this committee is to develop/maintain/ and update a hospital formulary (a listing of all drugs, by generic names, which are available in and utilized by the hospital pharmacy), oversee the operation and function of the hospital pharmacy, and monitor adverse drug reactions (A.D.R.) to medication of the hospitalized patient.

In light of the potential frequency of Adverse Drug Events in a hospital it behooves the hospitalized patient to be knowledgeable about the medication he/she utilizes (name, dose, frequency, description) and to be informed about new medication introduced. It also behooves the hospital to provide the patient with medication information, to take steps to check and review orders for medication as to their correctness and appropriateness (i.e., kind, dose, time, change), to conduct periodic reviews and assessments on medications given routinely over a period of time in order to check on necessity and efficacy, to develop procedures to minimize errors of omission or commission in drug prescription, manufacture, distribution, and dispensing.

How The Hospital Works: Other Professional Services

At the present time there are as many as 25 additional professional services available in our modern hospital beyond those described, depending on the size of the hospital and the range of its medical and surgical services. These other professional services can range for examples from respiratory care to social work to rehabilitation. Regardless of the number of these programs, they all have the following in common with each other. They each: function as a service to assist the physician in the diagnosis and treatment of the medical and surgical problems of the hospitalized patient; are provided by personnel who must meet the standards of education and training established for their profession/discipline; must meet the standards established for a hospital, as enunciated by accreditation, certifying and licensing bodies (national, state, local); are revenue producing

Skeletons in the Medical Closet
A Personal Story and a Professional Report

for the hospital as their charges can be billed to the patient (third party payor) directly; fall within the purview of the rules and regulations governing the medical staff of the hospital.

How A Hospital Works: It's "Watchdog" Activities

Of all the personnel and activities which ordinarily are viewed as administrative and management services within a hospital, there is a constellation of personnel (and their activities) who have a great impact on the safety, competence and quality of patient care provided the hospitalized patient. I am referring to: personnel who are seldom in direct contact with a patient, but whose activities are focused on monitoring and maintaining established standards of patient care and activities which include the programs of medical records and record keeping, patient representation, utilization review, quality assurance, risk management, infection control. These are "watchdog" activities of a hospital which are vital to patient assurance of safety and quality of services and which will be discussed in greater detail in the following chapter entitled Who Watches Physicians and Hospitals. These are activities which enable the hospital to meet the standards established for compliance with regulations for licensing and accreditation so that the hospital can receive payment from Medicare, Medicaid, Blue Cross/Blue Shield and other insurance carriers. These are activities of a hospital which are relevant to the identification of the failures in and of hospitals, such as unnecessary surgery, inappropriate admissions, inappropriate tests, medication errors, unanticipated death, errors of omission or commission, procedures conducted by insufficiently trained and inadequately supervised personnel, and malfunctioning equipment, but to mention a few.

Many of these "watch dog" activities have been carried out by hospitals for years. It is of import, however, to note that they became more meaningful during the past decade, and as a consequence of the stimulus produced by governmental

Meyer Sonis M.D.

regulations associated with the advent of Medicare and Medicaid, cost containment measures, increased enforcement of standards, public disclosures, scrutiny by third-party payors, malpractice suits, and public/consumer pressure. It is my belief that these activities of hospitals will have even greater impact on the future clinical care of the hospitalized patient because of the ultimate "pay off" from current developments (i.e., practice guidelines, clinical indicators, outcome studies) which will be referred to elsewhere. This "pay off" will hold the hospitals and their medical staffs accountable to explain and justify unnecessary and inappropriate admissions, mortality beyond the expected range, unanticipated and untoward outcomes of clinical and human care, over-utilization of costly procedures, hospital infections acquired by patients, variations in service utilization beyond established ranges, and clinical care which is outside the range of practice guidelines.

How A Hospital Works: Patient Representatives

Most modern hospitals in the United States have established a patient representative program wherein an employee associated with the administrative staff of the hospital serves as an advocate for the patient. As such an advocate, the patient representative is available to the hospitalized patient and/or his/her family to receive complaints regarding any aspect of patient care, whether it be about food, cleanliness, noise, discourteous personnel, and nursing or physician care. In larger hospitals this program can be a very organized one with a large staff employed by the hospital so that the patient representative not only can serve the patient as an advocate but also be of help to the patient's visitors in finding lodging and food if they are from out of town. In smaller hospitals such a program may be conducted by a volunteer staff.

Depending on the size of the patient representative program, the patient representatives may introduce themselves to every patient on admission and conduct an interview with the patient on the day of discharge in order to secure the views of the patient on his/her hospital experience. In some hospitals the patient representative may be available to the patient and/or the patient's family on request. In some hospitals, the patient or patient's family are requested to complete a formal questionnaire.

Though many such programs are put into place as a marketing tool of the hospital, it nevertheless can also serve as an avenue for the hospitalized patient (or family member) in sending a message to the senior level management and/or medical staff and/or Board of Directors of the hospital. It should be kept in mind that up until a few years ago such programs, if they existed, did not have much value for a patient because they were primarily "window dressing." More recently, as a consequence of consumer and marketing pressure, hospitals have begun to "serve" the patient in keeping with the as yet controversial Bill of Rights of Patients.

How A Hospital Works: Medical Records

The medical record (chart) of the hospitalized patient is the only legal and formal source of information and data which the hospital has about the patient and his/her medical or surgical problem(s). This information in the record can range from personal/ social/family information, past and current history of medical/surgical problem(s), reason for admission, medical/ surgical status on admission, what was done (studies, tests, procedures, physical examination, medication) and by whom and when and for what reasons and with what results and with what future outcome, and with what future medical/surgical plans. The medical record of the hospitalized patient becomes the one documented place of information and data about the diagnosis and treatment of the patient's problems on a continuing day by day/ hour by hour basis until discharge or death. The medical record becomes a legal statement for documenting the accountability of the hospital (its physicians and staff) about the actions taken on behalf of the hospitalized patient. It is the one place wherein every physician who has contact with a patient records his opinions and recommendations, every surgeon records the surgical procedure performed, every medication and procedure ordered for the patient is performed under a physician's recommendation and signature, every nurse who observes the patient and his/her behavior/dispenses medication to the patient/cares for the patient over a 24 hour period records this information, every consultant records his contact, the results of the pathology examination of tissues or organs removed during surgery are noted.

The medical record of the hospitalized patient becomes a confidential instrument between the patient and the hospital and though the record is the property of the hospital, the medical record (and the information therein) of the patient is available to the patient if requested, and can only be released to others with the written permission and/or at the request of the patient or his/her legal designee.

But most importantly, from the viewpoint of the failures in and of hospitals, the medical record has become the major tool utilized by the hospital and others (third party payors, governmental authorities, accreditation bodies) to monitor and evaluate the clinical care which has been rendered to the hospitalized patient. For examples: the hospital through its programs of quality assurance, utilization review, risk management and various committees (Medical Records, Medical Audit) utilizes the medical record to determine appropriateness of admission, efficacy of procedures utilized, completeness of records, appropriateness of surgery, adverse reactions to medications; third-party payors have the right to review medical records in order to determine or make decisions regarding hospital cost reimbursement; accreditation bodies, at the time of the accreditation process, require a random review of a sample of records in order to ascertain maintenance of standards.

Skeletons in the Medical Closet
A Personal Story and a Professional Report

Parenthetically it should be noted that the studies regarding medical errors (referred to in a previous chapter) relied totally on a review of medical records. It should be kept in mind that with the current advances in the information sciences, the advent of computerized medical record capabilities, and the increasing utilization of uniform medical record standardization, the medical record in the future will become an even more effective instrument by which to focus on failures in and of hospitals. For too long the hospital and its physicians have acted as if the medical record of the hospitalized patient was solely their property. This attitude is undergoing change in keeping with the increased emergence of a patient's right to the information in his/her medical record. In fact, as I have noted in my opening chapter to this book, I have long believed that every patient on discharge from the hospital should formally request a copy of their own hospital record for their files and future reference.

How The Hospital Works: Quality Improvement Programs

In Chapter Six of this book, entitled Who Watches The Doctors and Hospitals, detailed information will be given on those programs of a hospital which are aimed at assuring the safety, competency and quality of clinical care provided to a hospitalized patient. This will include the hospital programs such as Risk Management, Utilization Review, Quality Assurance, which take place routinely behind the scenes of clinical care in all of our hospitals. The activities of these programs seldom directly involve or are known to the hospitalized patient but nevertheless serve the purpose of having "someone" looking over the "shoulder of" the patient himself/herself, all of the human hands providing clinical and human care, the various procedures performed on the hospitalized patient.

CHAPTER SIX

WHO WATCHES THE DOCTOR AND HOSPITAL

Self Monitoring by Physicians

From time immemorial society has entrusted the physician himself or herself to watch over his/her effectiveness and results of patient care. Society assumed that the physician would do no harm to the patient, identify, prevent and minimize ineffective and inappropriate patient care and errors, place the interest of the patient over his or her own interest. This responsibility of a physician to be self critical and self-policing has been inculcated into the physician beginning with his/her medical school education and continuing through his/her career of lifetime learning.

As noted elsewhere, once the physician received his or her license to practice medicine, the physician was generally on his or her own in being accountable for decisions and actions regarding the care of a patient. Within the private office of the physician, the physician did not have any one looking over his shoulder regarding what he/she was doing with or to the patient, except in the event of a patient complaint to an appropriate authority, or in the event of a patient's death requiring a coroner's inquiry, or in the event of readmission of the patient to a hospital in order to correct a complication/effect of the physician's previous care as reported in the Harvard Studies. Prior to WWII, though hospitalization of a patient by a physician did increase the chance of having other physicians available to look over the shoulder of the admitting physician (such as, through peer review in hospital conferences, autopsy reports, tissue reports following surgery), attending physicians generally were comparatively "free" of oversight due to the physician fiefdom in the hospital.

Skeletons in the Medical Closet
A Personal Story and a Professional Report

Because of the limited availability of reliable information regarding the effectiveness of a physician's self-policing efforts in the care of their patients within their "private" offices, it has been and is difficult to answer this question with any degree of certainty. In a 1996 report, entitled Questionable Doctors published by the Public Citizen Health Report, the report states "yet for too long the State and Federal Government Agencies chartered to protect us from those no longer fit to hold the privilege of a medical license have fallen down on the job. Many state medical boards and other regulatory agencies have either entirely failed to catch doctors guilty of incompetence, drunkenness or patient abuse, or have let them get away with their mistakes".

Fortunately the greatest strides which have been made in monitoring the effectiveness of physicians in their care of patients (and will be referred to elsewhere in this chapter) has taken place within the setting of the modern hospital.

Since WW II, and at an increasing pace more recently, hospitals have undergone major changes in their acceptance of a need for implementation of programs to monitor the outcome of hospital care of patients and to monitor and police physicians and all other caregivers in their rendering of their medical care. There can be no doubt that this increased pace of changes in hospitals has been an outgrowth of the changing scene of health care delivery, including that of an informed public. With these changes in and by hospitals much more reliable data is now available regarding outcome of medical care in hospitals, hospital mistakes and physician errors. Some of these changes in "policing" patient care by hospitals have been referred to by me in the previous chapter on The Hospital Industry, but others of these changes will be reported in the remainder of this chapter.

Meyer Sonis M.D.

Monitoring by the Patient Satisfaction Program of Hospitals

This program is usually staffed by social workers and/or psychologists and many times is an offshoot of the patient representative program referred to in the previous chapter. The Patient Satisfaction Program is aimed at securing the opinion (via interview or survey) of the hospitalized patient (or family), at the time of discharge (or a few days post discharge) from the hospital, regarding their satisfaction with the personal (food, lodging, housekeeping), medical (physicians, nurses, technicians), and the business aspects of their hospital care. The responses to the survey are analyzed and the results are tabulated and reported to the appropriate medical staff committee and administration of the hospital. Through this means, "clues" are gleaned about adverse events, medical injuries and hospital mistakes. In a well designed and conducted and fiscally supported study (R. W. Johnson Foundation) it was demonstrated in a Boston hospital that such a program could be of value in providing meaningful information about the potential of adverse events occurring to hospitalized patients. However, in most of such programs, and because of the methods utilized, the value is limited primarily to the personal and business care aspects of patient care and not to the quality of patient care.

Monitoring By The Utilization Review Program (U.R.) Of Hospitals

This program is usually staffed by a non-physician clinician (such as a nurse, nurse practitioner). As shown in the organizational chart of the hospital (see previous chapter) the U.R. Program is an administrative unit of the hospital. These programs have primarily been initiated as an outgrowth of cost containment policies of third party payors (such as. Medicare). These programs were focused primarily as a means for the hospital to: secure prior approval of a patient's admission to the hospital from the designated third party payor; secure from the third party payor the designated length of hospital stay for the patient according to the designated admitting diagnosis; minimize and monitor inappropriate admissions, inappropriate or unneeded procedures, unneeded medication, inappropriate patient discharge, and all in keeping with the criteria of the third party payor regarding reimbursement; periodically review the patient's medical record in order to see that there is sufficient documentation of the reason for the patient's remaining in the hospital and receiving treatment, in order to assure payment by the payor. This review of the patient's daily record by the U.R. Program, while the patient is in the hospital, is called a concurrent review since it parallels the patient's stay in the hospital. In conducting this record review the nurse abstractor of the U.R. Program does not communicate with the patient nor examine the patient nor formally record her/his information in the official medical record of the patient, so that nothing of the U.R. Program data on the hospitalized patient becomes a part of the official medical records. In conducting the medical record review the nurse abstractor maintains a record of his/her review, leaves notes for the physician to "prompt" the physician to do more documentation in the record to justify the need for continued hospitalization. The findings and data of such a U.R. review are called to the attention of the appropriate committee of the medical staff and the administration of the hospital. It is the medical staff and only the medical staff which can mete out sanctions (in keeping with their by-law regulations) on a physician for infractions reported by the U.R. program.

Even though the nurse abstractors of the U.R. program are capable of and in a very good position, because of their daily medical record review, to focus on signs and symptoms and laboratory reports of the patient which might be a signal to a potential "bad" thing occurring, most U.R. Programs stay tightly focused on the business and fiscal end of care. However, some hospitals have taken steps to enlarging the objectives of their

U.R. Programs so that the nurse abstractor can utilize standardized screen criteria for potential adverse events in their review of the medical record.

Monitoring By The Risk Management Program Of A Hospital

This hospital program, as displayed in the pictorial organizational chart of a hospital, is an administrative program of the hospital, with accountability to the management of the hospital, as well as to the appropriate committee of the medical staff. Ordinarily the personnel of this program are staff who have been specifically trained to be a risk manager, and may be social workers, nurses, psychologists.

The purpose of the risk management program is, just as its name suggests, to identify hospitalized patients who, because of an alleged negligent medical injury to them by a person or persons providing medical care, potentially may place the hospital and hospital personnel at risk of a legal suit or action. The risk managers serve as "damage control" personnel. These patients are called to the attention of the risk managers through incident reports by hospital personnel or by other monitoring programs of the hospital or by patients or their family complaining about alleged accidents or adverse events or inappropriate patient care.

Ordinarily the risk manager does not directly become involved in the patient's care or have contact with the patient, though they may question the patient about their alleged complaint. The risk manager does review the medical record of the patient, but usually does not make an official note of this in the medical record of the patient. The reason for this is obvious. The risk managers conduct a thorough investigation of the incident/complaint and maintain internal records (not available to the patient or patient's family) of their findings. In their investigation the risk manager may collaborate with the personnel of the hospital involved in the alleged incident, the legal staff of the hospital, the insurance company serving the hospital, the appropriate committee of the medical staff, the management of the hospital. The risk managers also provide educational programs to the hospital staff regarding the risk management program and also provide guidance and counseling to hospital staff involved in such incidents. In some hospitals the risk managers culminate their investigation by estimating the potential financial cost to the hospital for damages if the "suit" is successful for the patient.

As can be surmised from my comments the risk management programs as with the U.R. Program, because of its concurrent review of a medical record while the patient is hospitalized, can potentially serve as a watch dog for monitoring the potential of adverse events occurring to a hospitalized patient. Unfortunately because of their focus on "guarding" the hospital and its personnel from the risk of a legal action, the risk management program falls far short of also serving the interests of the patient.

Monitoring By The Infectious Control Program Of A Hospital

This program of the hospital is operated as an extension of the Department of Infectious Disease of a hospital and the appropriate committee of the medical staff, with accountability to the Department and to the management of the hospital. The objective of this program is to monitor the potential occurrences of infections to hospitalized patients, and in selected situations to report such occurrences to the appropriate public health officials (local, state, federal) and to institute steps to curtail the spread of infections between patients.

Though such programs are not usually viewed as watchdog programs, they do and can serve a most important purpose in identifying and protecting a hospitalized patient from the consequences of acquiring a nosocomial (hospital) infection, a

Meyer Sonis M.D.

wound infection following surgery, urinary infection from urinary procedures and equipment. It is programs such as these which assure sterile conditions in the operating room, in the equipment utilized for internal (invasive) procedures (biopsy, laporoscope, bronchoscope, tubes, catheters). Again, as with the Quality Assurance and Risk Management Programs, this program does not communicate with the patient directly or indirectly through a note in the patient';s medical record, except as reported in results of their laboratory studies. In most cases, if there is an infection or suspected infection, the infectious disease specialist comes into play as a "formal" consultant.

Monitoring By The Quality Assurance Program Of A Hospital

Currently all accredited hospitals have instituted the operation of a quality assurance program within their institution. This program usually serves as a distinct administrative unit of the hospital (see pictorial chart) with administrative accountability to the management of the hospital and professional accountability to the medical staff of the hospital. These programs are usually under the direction of a nurse who has been specifically trained in quality assurance methods and procedures and are staffed by nurses who serve as reviewers (abstractors) of medical records. In some hospitals a physician may be employed to serve as director of the quality assurance program.

The major impetus for the development of these programs in our modern hospital can be directly linked to the climate which has surrounded and is surrounding the delivery of health care in the 70's, 80's and 90's. I am referring to a climate which includes at least the following factors: the pressure on the academic medical community (medical center teaching hospitals) to undertake and conduct studies into the effectiveness outcome of medical interventions (i.e. medication, procedures, surgery); the dissatisfaction with the "self" policing measures of physicians

Skeletons in the Medical Closet
A Personal Story and a Professional Report

and hospitals; the emergence of federal and state mandated requirements on medical care providers to monitor and report on medical services which are provided to patients and paid for by public monies.

Suffice to say that these programs of Quality Assurance or Improvement have become the lynch pin for the monitoring objective of a hospital to assure a patient that the services rendered them are safe, competent and of a quality in keeping with established standards. The parameters utilized by the quality assurance programs in hospitals (other health care organization) have been developed as integral to the process and procedures for accreditation of a hospital by the Joint Commission on Accreditation of Health Care Organizations. These parameters for quality assurance programs have undergone continuous revision, in keeping with the increasing emergence of newer knowledge about outcome of medical care. The "teeth" which have helped to push hospitals to abide by these standards of "accreditation" is to be found in the relationship between a hospital's accreditation approval and receiving reimbursement from third party payors.

The functions of the quality assurance program of a hospital are multiple: to monitor the outcome of medical care to a hospitalized patient, i.e. its safety, competence and quality; to monitor ("police") the performance of the physicians who are rendering medical care to the hospitalized patient; to develop the data and information required for a report on the quality of medical care rendered to the management/the medical staff of the hospital/appropriate authorities as called for.

In carrying out its functions the quality assurance program conducts a review of the medical record of a hospitalized patient following discharge from or death in the hospital. This review is called a retrospective review as differentiated from the concurrent review of the U.R. program. In carrying out its review of the hospital record of the patient the program relies on methods, procedures, protocols which have been developed and

Meyer Sonis M.D.

continually refined by the extraordinary scientific and clinical knowledge now available as a consequence of outcome studies, management information systems, uniform clinical reporting by hospitals on hospitalized patients as required by federal and state government, screening instruments which are able to measure and score adverse events/severity of illness/sentinel events. By this review the quality assurance program is in a position to generate profiles on the patient care rendered such as demographic/ clinical characteristics, the services provided and procedures utilized, the results of clinical studies, the personnel who are rendering the services, the costs of services provided and the outcome of patient care. By this review of the hospital record of the patient, the quality assurance program can render profiles on the physicians rendering care, such as physicians who tend to have higher mortality rates than others, physicians who tend to have more complications following procedures, physicians who tend to have more adverse events occurring to patients. The validity and reliability of utilizing the hospital record as a review source, for data and information to measure the safety, competence and quality of medical care rendered, has now been more than amply demonstrated by the Harvard Study Group and others, as briefly described in the previous chapters.

As with the programs of utilization review and infectious control, the quality assurance program does not directly have contact with a hospitalized patient nor is any information about the findings of the quality assurance program noted in the record of the hospitalized patient.

Monitoring By The Medical Staff Of A Hospital

In the hospital of today the Medical Staff, with functions described in the previous chapter on the Hospital Industry, does and can play a valued role in the "policing" of a physician in his/her rendering of safe, competent and quality of medical care. In discharge of this role the Medical Staff utilizes its various committees, the information and data it receives from the various "monitoring" programs (of the hospital) which report to the medical staff, the incident reports which are called to its attention, the information and data about a physician it receives from a regulatory agency/a licensing authority/the National Practitioner Data Bank, the record of attendance of a physician at continuing education programs, and other such sources, which all serve as eyes and ears for the medical staff in looking over the physician's shoulder. It is through these various means that a judgement can be made about the ability of a physician to perform as a surgeon or radiologist and an assessment can be secured about a physician's conduct and behavior. It is through such means that a decision can be made about the need for sanctions against a physician for infractions and violations. Though the current watchdog purpose of the medical staff is a far cry from the old boys club of the past, it is still difficult for the public to know about these internal findings of the Medical Staff regarding a physician of the medical staff.

Monitoring Of Physicians By State Board Of Medical Licensure

In each state of the United States a State Board of Medical Licensure or its equivalent is mandated by the state government to grant a medical license for a physician to practice in that state upon successful completion of their written/oral examination. This examination is intended to test the acquisition by the candidate of the appropriate knowledge required to provide safe, competent and quality of medical care to a patient. Thus these State Boards become the first line of defense for monitoring the ability of a physician to render appropriate medical care in keeping with standards established.

It is oftentimes forgotten that these same State Boards also have a legal responsibility to identify physicians who have violated their privilege to practice medicine because of below standard medical practice and/or behavior and actions. In keeping with this authority the State Boards have the legal power to sanction these physicians, if found guilty of the violation, and to disseminate this information to the public. Information about the various actions of State Boards is collected, analyzed and disseminated by the national organization of the Federation of State Medical Boards (representative of each State Board of Medical License).

In a most excellent report referred to previously (called Questionable Doctors) a report was given by the authors on their findings of a study of physicians whose medical care or conduct was substandard enough to be cited by a state medical disciplinary board or Medicare or the Federal Drug Enforcement Agency. Of "13,000 doctors cited for offenses and who were disciplined: 12% were cited for substandard care or incompetence; 11% for misprescribing or over prescribing of drugs; 15% for a criminal conviction; 9% for drug and alcohol abuse; 8% for professional misconduct; less than 1% for Medicare fraud," but to mention a few. In this report it was noted that sanctions were comparatively mild, for examples, "21%" of these physicians were given probation, 10% had their licenses revoked, 8% were fined." It has also been reported that these sanctions do not stop a physician from practice in another state. More recently pressures have begun to emerge for putting more "teeth" into this first line of defense through mandating a re-examination of a physician by state board medical licensing examination periodically (every seven years). In this reexamination, it was felt that consideration could be given to a more thorough examination of the physician's medical practice itself and not simply an examination of his/her "knowledge." This latter consideration is an outgrowth of the fact that sufficient data is available to suggest that continuing education as currently provided in lectures/conferences does not materially change physician behavior or action or medical practice. Canada has led the way in this reform by basing the examination for a

Skeletons in the Medical Closet
A Personal Story and a Professional Report

medical license on the cases and records of a physician's practice.

Monitoring Of Physicians: By Physician Specialty Accreditation Boards

Another line of defense, for assurance of the public that a physician specialist has the ability to practice specialized medicine and surgery in keeping with standards of safety, competence and quality, is that of the various certifying specialty boards referred to in the chapter on The Physician Industry. It is these certifying boards which both monitor the credibility of the various training programs to educate and train a specialty practitioner and the credibility of a practitioner as having successfully passed the requisite certifying examination. However, it is to be remembered that undertaking physician specialist training is a decision on the part of a physician, since it is not mandated by law as is securing a license to practice medicine. For this reason, the certifying boards do not have the mandating authority to monitor the practice performance of all of its certified specialists or the practice performance of self designated specialists or the practice performance of those physician specialists who do not take the certifying examination. Since several studies have demonstrated a positive correlation between the successful passage of a certifying examination by a physician and rating by peers of clinical competence of a physician specialist, certifying examinations can be a most useful index of a physician's ability to practice sound medical care.

As a consequence of these studies and reports, questions have been raised about a one time lifetime certification of a physician specialist by a specialty board, similar to the questions regarding a one time lifetime state board license to practice medicine. In keeping with these questions, federal and state legislation has been proposed to require physician recertification

Meyer Sonis M.D.

and recredentialling periodically. To date 19 of the 25 physician specialty boards have begun such consideration, and some have taken steps to address the issues of recredentialling of physicians as a basis for reimbursement of physician specialist services. In an excellent article (1991) regarding these issues of recredentialling, the author notes that the "arguments for recredentialling of physicians, together with the abundant examples of overuse/underuse/inappropriate use of diagnostic and operating procedures and medications, have given prominence to quality assurance in the public debate about the American health care system." It should be parenthetically noted that the bold studies of the Harvard Group attest to the forward thinking of the State of New York.

Monitoring Of Hospitals by Joint Commission on Accreditation of Health Care Organizations

The Joint Commission on Accreditation of Health Care organizations (JCAHCO), formerly known as Joint Commission of Accreditation of Hospitals (JCAH), was founded in 1959 as a voluntary non-profit organization to develop and establish standards for hospitals and to evaluate compliance of hospitals with these standards. With the expansion of its purposes to also now include healthcare networks, health plans, home care programs, ambulatory care and outpatient services, nursing homes, programs for mental health/chemical dependency/ rehabilitation/clinical laboratories and most recently physician offices, the JCAHCO now evaluates and accredits 18,000 different health care organizations and programs in the U.S during the course of a year.

Though this organization is a voluntary one, in that a hospital voluntarily seeks accreditation, the reason which make health care organizations "volunteer" to be evaluated by and maintain JCAHCO standards is to be found in the need of the hospital for this approval if it is to be reimbursed by Medicare

Skeletons in the Medical Closet
A Personal Story and a Professional Report

and Medicaid. The accreditation process for approval of a health care organization is initiated by submission of an extensive application by a health care organization and is followed by an on site inspection by a survey team from the JCAHCO. During the on site inspection, the JCAHCO staff: interview key governing/ key department/administrative personnel/programs/ service personnel of the hospital; review a random selection of patient records from each service of the organization; review fiscal audits; review the medical staff by laws and records, minutes of meetings and internal reports; meet with house staff; tour and inspect the physical plant. If approval is granted it can be done for a three year period, or a one year provisional time pending time to correct deficiencies found. In order to supplement these periodic site visits, a sample (5%) of the health care organizations are selected for unannounced visits. Additionally unannounced for-cause surveys are conducted in response to serious incidents related to the health and safety of patients or staff or reported complaints.

Even though the JCAHCO has an important role to play in standard setting and monitoring of standards at the health care organizations, it's record in monitoring the compliance of these organizations to assure patient safety, competence in medical care and quality of medical care has not been the most satisfactory indeed. Further, its record of making the information public has left much to be desired. In response to these criticisms the JCAHCO has initiated several new or expanded directions, namely: to review the performance of health care organizations on a quarterly basis rather than a three year basis, in order to search out factors at the hospital which may impact negatively on the outcome of patient care or survival; to incorporate criteria into its accreditation process which can measure outcomes; to render periodic "public" reports.

Meyer Sonis M.D.

Monitoring Of Hospitals By Other Organizations

The National Committee for Quality Assurance (NCQA) was formed in 1979 by and for the managed care industry and Group Health Association, partly in response to the considerations by the federal government regarding the need for governmental plans to monitor the managed care industry. From 1979 to 1990 the NCQA continued its work on developing measures of quality assurance. In 1990, the NCQA became an independent, nonprofit organization chartered to develop standards of quality assurance and to monitor compliance with these standards of health care programs, such as HMO's and various health plans. The NCQA has now emerged as a leader in the field of reviewing quality assurance programs and monitoring the performance of the 650 HMO's in the U.S. As of the present, 53% of these HMO's have been reviewed and given accreditation by the NCQA for a three year or one year period of provisional approval. Of utmost importance to the issue of utilizing measures by which to more reliably monitor the outcome of services rendered by a health plan and its physicians, the NCQA itself developed an instrument called a Health Plan Employees Data and Information Set (HEDIS) which is now in its 54th revision. This HEDIS instrument, more than many other measure of outcome, has been able to become standardized as an assessment tool to address practice performance of a provider. This instrument focuses on: the practice of over utilized, under utilized, inappropriate procedures and medications; established practice guidelines of care in disease/illness (such as myocardial infarction, stroke, tonsillitis, ear infections in children). It is the opinion of leaders in the field that the success of NCQA (including its HEDIS) is impacting on and is being utilized by all other similar monitoring organizations (including the JCAHCO).

The Foundation For Accountability (FACCT) was established in 1995 as an outgrowth of coalition efforts by government, public advocate groups, labor and industry. It is a non profit organization with the purpose of securing and reporting of medical care data and information to the consumer of such services. FACCT has been developing and using rigorous science based measures for assessing quality. To date FACCT has reported on eight quality assessment tools for each of the following, diabetes, adult asthma, cancer, major depression, health risk behavior, health status of people 65 years of age, and consumer satisfaction with health plans.

Monitoring Of Physicians And Hospitals By Governmental Authorities

With the enactment of federal laws to govern the Medicare and Medicaid programs, the federal and state governments mandated not only the delivery of and payment for health care services to the eligible populations but also mandated the monitoring of these services rendered by providers (health care organizations, physicians, others).

In order to carry out the monitoring or policing of providers who deliver services to the mandated populations, the law governing the Medicare and Medicaid Programs (in 1972) called for the development of independent non-profit organizations called Professional Standards Review Organization (PSRO). The PSRO by contract with the governmental authority for the Medicare program was given the authority to serve as the "watchdog" of hospitals, doctors and other providers. The PSRO, numbering 195, were located in various regions of the U.S. and were given responsibilities for overseeing the providers in the designated area. In order to assure the ability of a PSRO to gain support of the medical profession and to employ local doctors to conduct peer review of the actions of other doctors in their region, the operation of a PSRO was to be vested in a physician directed governing body. Though the PSRO's were given authority to achieve these mandated objectives and to recommend sanctions if appropriate, the record of these PSRO's has shown that at best the PSRO was a comparatively poor watch dog of the services and providers. The PSRO had become too much of a monitor of "costs" of services and not enough of a monitor of the providers which rendered the services..

In 1982, Congress did away with the PSRO initiative in order to replace them with 54 Peer Review Organizations (PRO), mostly defined by state boundaries. The PRO was an independent profit or non-profit organization which would be under contract with the Medicare trust fund (i.e. to avoid uncertainties of congressional funding) to carry out their mandated objectives and sanction authority. These contracts, which detailed the terms of the objectives, were renewable after two years, pending success of the PRO in meeting its stated objectives..

The various objectives, which the PRO's were to achieve during their two year contract period, were called the "scope of work" (1984-1986) and reflected the need of the PRO to monitor the effectiveness of the newly developed Prospective Payment System (PPS) of the Medicare Program, wherein a provider hospital would be paid a standardized fee for patient services provided based on the estimated average costs for hospitalization of a patient with a diagnosis according to a designated Diagnosis Related Group (DRG). Thus, the first scope of work called for by the PRO was focused on: an assessment of the appropriateness and necessity for hospital admissions; the readmissions and transfers of hospital patients (in order to identify possibly premature discharge); the accuracy of a hospital's coding of a patient's DRG (in order to determine if overpayments were made by Medicare); patients whose length of hospitalization exceeded the length of hospitalization called for by a given DRG (in order to document the need for a higher payment).

The second scope of work (1986-1988) for the PRO was to focus on the development and use of generic screening criteria to monitor the quality of services rendered. These screens were procedural check lists which a nurse could utilize in her/his review of medical records of a hospitalized patient. The screens referred to here are very similar to the kind of screens utilized (and referred to earlier) by the Harvard Group Studies in order to identify potential problems in medical care, such as premature discharge of an unstabilized patient, an unanticipated death, nosocomial infections, the need for a patient return to surgery.

The third scope of work for a PRO (1988-1991) focused on areas previously called for in an earlier scope of work but with a more intense focus on the review of all preadmission records of patients who required any of ten procedures (certain invasive procedures and risks), the newly developed Quality Intervention Plan (QIP) of the Medicare Program (a demerit system for doctors, hospitals, other providers), developing statistical profiles on providers (such as hospitals, physicians and others) regarding rates of mortality, readmissions, admission denials, generic screen failures.

The fourth scope of work (1991-1996) prescribed for the PRO called for a decrease in the number of medical records to be reviewed (as called for in previous scope of works) while paying increased attention to the Health Care Quality Improvement Program (HCQIP) initiated and developed by the governmental authority for the Medicare Program. The HCQIP "represents a movement away from individual case review by a PRO towards the investigation and evaluation of changes in patterns of care and outcome in services provided." The HCQIP intended to compare patterns of care and outcome between various providers utilizing one centralized standardized data base.

The current scope of work prescribed for the PRO (1996-1998) opened the door for the extension of PRO monitoring to other than hospitals and their physicians, such as Managed Care Organizations, physician offices, rehabilitation programs, nursing homes. In this monitoring the PRO will rely on the HEDIS Scale (see comments under National Committee For Quality Assurance). A spokesperson for the Health Care

Meyer Sonis M.D.

Financing Administration (HCFA) recently stated that "we primarily have been a bill payer. But now we will be a beneficiary centered purchaser."

It is to be remembered that under federal law the teeth behind the PRO (as a monitoring function) is its authority to recommended to the contractor (Federal Government) fines or suspensions against physicians and other providers if they have "grossly or flagrantly" violated their obligations to Medicare patients. They can also recommend sanctions if a practitioner provider has failed to comply with quality standards established. These sanction recommendations, if approved by the HCFA, can only be carried out by the Inspector General of the Department of Health and Human Services. From data available, for the period of 1985-1990, PRO's submitted 224 sanction recommendations to the IG resulting in exclusion from Medicare reimbursement of 95 doctors and 1 hospital, in a fine of 25 physicians and 2 hospitals, in the rejection of the recommendation of 87 cases. From other reliable data secured by a review of 270 hospital cases through the Super PRO (monitors all other PRO) the Super PRO questioned the quality of service in 10% of these cases; but more importantly the PRO's involved agreed that they missed half of the problems they should have detected.

Despite the valid criticism which has been leveled at the monitoring efforts of the Medicare Program (because of the influence of politics, pressures of the organized medical lobby, avoidance of controversy) the Medicare Program nevertheless is to be given credit for it's influence in supporting the need for watch dogs over hospitals, doctors, health care organization and the need for continued improvement of instruments to measure outcome, effectiveness, safety and competence in patient care.

Skeletons in the Medical Closet
A Personal Story and a Professional Report

Monitoring Of Physicians By: The National Practitioner Data Bank

With the enactment of the Health Care Quality Improvement Act of 1986 (HCQIA) by Congress, a legal base and a national reporting system was established to improve the ability of the health professions to "police" themselves. Without belaboring the point, or reiterating the details referred to elsewhere in this book, the need for such action by Congress grew out of increasing concern that the medical profession was manifesting problems with its ability to assure safe, competent and quality of medical care rendered by physicians. Such concerns were based on the continuing lack of information about the adverse behavior of physicians, the extent of medical mal-practice, the tracking of physicians who may not be competent. Reports by the Inspector General's Office over two decades confirmed the serious limitations of verification capabilities of State Boards of Medical Licensure regarding aberrant behavior and practice of physicians, the inadequacy of physician credential verification methods, the laxity in "oversight" capabilities for monitoring physicians.

Because of the heavy reliance on professional peer review activities in order to monitor the medical care rendered by physicians and hospitals, Congress maintained in the passage of this act that steps must be taken to protect physicians from liability in their role as a peer review physician and to protect the quality assurance programs of hospitals from liability. Under the Act, Congress granted immunity to physicians participating in peer review activities and to the quality assurance programs of a hospital. Under this Act Congress also established the National Practitioner Data Bank (NPDB) to assure that information used in the peer review process would be accurate, complete, available to selected parties and confidential. The act mandated reports to the NPDB from hospitals (and other such sources) about malpractice payments and adverse actions taken against a physician (such as sanctions by a State Medical Board, sanctions against a physician's clinical privileges at a hospital, or sanctions against membership of a physician in a professional society). The act also mandated that health care organizations (hospitals) must secure information and clearance from the NPDB regarding potential employment and granting of clinical privileges to a physician. In the first year of its operation, the NPDB (1990-1991) had received reports on 14,000 physicians of whom 11,000 were reported because of medical malpractice payments, 1,500 for license sanction, 750 for privilege sanction, 17 for sanction by a professional society. During that time almost 800,000 queries were made (primarily from hospitals about physicians). In a 1992 publication about this National Practitioner Data Bank, the author indicated "the data generated by the NPDB is providing global information of the kind never available before."

Monitoring of Physicians and Hospitals: By The Legal Profession

My comments in this section are intended to serve as a supplement to comments I have previously made in this book on the subject of medical malpractice and the legal process.

From the information which is available it would seem that the "policing" role of the legal profession, in looking over the shoulder of doctors and hospitals, is almost exclusively that of either defending the doctor and hospital against claims of fraud and medical negligence or that of accusing them at the behest of others of fraud and negligence.

At its best this "policing" role of the legal profession has really only served but a few of the total number of patients who have received substandard medical care; at its worst this "policing" role has not only not deterred continued rendering of substandard medical care but it has also aided and abetted the medical conspiracy of silence. In fact, the policing of doctors

Skeletons in the Medical Closet
A Personal Story and a Professional Report

and hospitals could better be served by the reform of the adversary system of the legal process towards a more "unbiased and neutral" system of "no-fault insurance" so that all aggrieved parties of substandard medical care could secure compensation commensurate with damages incurred.

Further, the legal profession can serve a role in policing doctors and hospitals by supporting the need for an increase in legal advocacy for the public good. Such advocates can: assure the adherence of the doctors and hospitals to the bill of rights of patients; penetrate the wall of hidden information about a patient which is not made available to the patient by doctors and hospitals; undertake class actions for the consumer patient (and not simply for the lucrative action against industrial polluters or the tobacco industry) who is not receiving the care which is adjudged to be "standard care" for patients with diabetes, hypertension, angina, cataracts, disorders of the elderly or young.

Monitoring Of Physicians And Hospitals: By The Lay Public

In concluding this chapter on Who Watches The Doctor? and Who Watches The Hospital?, I can think of no more fitting way to do this than by adding the lay public to the list of potential monitors of watchdogs of doctors and hospitals. I believe it is mandatory to do so because as consumers of medical care they have the most to gain by medical care which is safe, competent and of a quality to meet standards and the most to lose if it is not.

Though the lay public may see themselves as consumers of medical care, they may not see themselves as having any influence on the decisions and actions which doctors and hospitals make and take in rendering medical care. The lay public must be reminded of the power which they can exert on those responsible for provision of medical care if, as consumers of medical care, they are informed patients; if, as consumers of medical care, they realize that they are ultimately the payors for medical care; if, as consumers of medical care, they approach the medical care they receive with an attitude of buyer beware.

If ever the consumer of medical care needed to be reminded of the timeliness of the role which they must play in securing quality in the medical care they receive, attention must be called to the slow pace of changes and slight gains which have been made by doctors and hospitals in rendering quality of medical care to all patients, the slow change of pace and slight gains which have been made by the doctor and hospital watchers in their ability to protect the consumer of medical care from unsafe, incompetent and sub-standard care.

To illustrate the timeliness of this reminder to the consumer of medical care, and to emphasize the comments I have made, I am calling attention to several quotes from recent articles published in several Consumer Reports (September/October, 1998). Of especial interest in this latter article is the fact that the Health Policy Editor of the Consumer Reports, who wrote the article is also a member of the Board of Directors of the monitoring organization described previously, namely, the NCQA.

"If you are looking for an HMO (Health Maintenance Organization) this fall, you can probably find the cheapest plan, but you cannot find the best one... one whose doctors always make timely and correct diagnoses, choose effective treatment, avoid mistakes. That is because there are no good comparisons of health plans on measures like these. There are no exemplary models of health plans or providers who deliver care that is uniformly and consistently of the highest quality, which was noted by the prestigious Institute of Medicine (IOM) of the National Academy of Sciences." "There are major and extensive quality problems in American medicine and they are spread across all delivery systems. The problem is not managed care but quality of care." "It is disappointing then, that of more than 300 health care plans we contacted, only 63 were willing to disclose anything about their quality initiatives. Most of what they did tell us described activities which were mediocre."

In order to prepare themselves for their role as watchdogs of the medical care they seek and receive, the consumer of medical care must become an informed consumer and patient. He or she must become knowledgeable about the various public advocacy organizations which are focused on the delivery of health care, the medical services for the elderly/young/and uninsured, the medical services for specific diseases/genetic diseases, and which serve as "public" lobbyists in the political arena of government and of the medical-hospital industries. As an informed patient, he or she must become knowledgeable about their own health, their family's health, their familial disorders or health problems, their body and its functions, their medications and their drug reactions, their own medical and hospital records. He or she must become knowledgeable about doctors and hospitals in general, their own doctors and hospitals, medical procedures and their benefits and risks. He or she must become informed and knowledgeable and able to ask questions of their doctors and hospitals and all medical caregivers regarding the care they receive. He or she must secure and become knowledgeable about the public information and data available to the public about doctors and hospitals, and about the "score card" records of outcomes, cost,, effectiveness, under/over/misuse of procedures. Finally, he or she must avail themselves of the wealth of resources now available to and from which the informed consumer and patient can secure the knowledge they seek.

Meyer Sonis M.D.

<u>EPILOGUE</u>

On my completion of this manuscript, which has taken me nine years to do, it is time to acknowledge all of those who have been of help.

To begin with I owe a great debt of gratitude to the information and data which I relied on to report. Some of this information and data, though older in time, did not have to be updated since it is as valid today as it was in the past. Some information and data, when updated, was by degree more of the same and helped to confirm tentative information of the past. Some of the information and data was groundbreaking and has set the tone for the future. To all of these persons I do thank them for their creativity in shedding light publicly on matters of concern to all who seek and secure medical care.

Secondly, I must call attention to other physicians, who have hurt and participated in my studies and who told me personal stories of their encounters with the skeletons in the medical closet. For this my thanks.

Third, I must thank my colleague and personal physician, Dr. Ralph Auchenbach, for the example he sets as the last angry physician who fights for good patient care and for patients to be informed.

Also, I must thank my two sons, and daughter for their waiting to see this book and to Elva and Dotty for their patience in typing and retyping.

Fourth, my thanks to Betty and Chick for their friendship with Anne and me and for their comfort of me during my dark days.

APPENDIX A

BIBLIOGRAPHIC REFERENCES

CHAPTER ONE: A Personal Story

Weinmar-Lear, M. (1980). Heart Sounds. Simon & Schuster, N.Y.

Mondel, H.N. (1986). How Physicians Get Their Care. Postgraduate Medicine, 79, 3.

Scientific American Medicine. (1988). Chapters on Pulmonary Infection, Infectious Disease of Gram Negative Bacilli. Scientific American, N.Y.

Stanford Surgical Department, Stanford University. (1988). Manual of Post Operative Management in Adult Cardiac Surgery. Williams & Wilkins, N.Y.

Bone, R. (1989). Sepsis syndrome. Critical Care Medicine, 17, 5, p. 389.

Personal Communication. (1989). Hospital medical record from X Hospital on patient A.C.S.

Personal Communication. (1990). Consultant reports from critical care specialist and pulmonologist. Review of hospital record on patient A.C.S.

Personal Communication. (1994). Expert witness report of physician specialist on infectious diseases. Review of hospital record on patient A.C.S.

Personal Communication. (1995). Reports of medical experts for defense attorney.

Review of hospital record on patient A.C.S.

Sonis, M. (1995). A Doctor Who Hurts. Adams Press, Chicago, IL ISBNo.9650533-0-X.

Parello, J. (1995). Mechanism of septic shock. New Engl J Med, 328, 20.

Vidmar, N. (1995). Medical Malpractice and the American Jury. University of Michigan Press Ann Arbor, MI.

Gilbert, S. (1995). Wrongful Death. W. W. Norton & Co., NY.

Fagan, J.Y. (1996). Nosocomial Pneumonia and Mortality among Patients in Intensive Care. JAMA, 275, 11, p. 866.

Allegheny County Local Rules of Court. (1997). Pittsburgh, Allegheny County Law Library.

The Empty Bench. (1998). Pittsburgh Post Gazette, February 15, 1998.

CHAPTER TWO: Medical Injuries, Medical Errors, Hospital Mistakes

Smith, J.W., et. al.. (1966). Studies on the epidemiology of adverse drug events.Ann Intern Medicine, 65, p. 629.

Couch, N.P., et. al. (1981). The anatomy and economics of surgical mishaps. N Engl J Med, 304, p. 634.

Friedman, M. (1982). Iatrogenic disease: a growing epidemic. Postgraduate Medicine, 71, p.128.

Nash, D.T. (1985). Medical Mayhem. Walker & Company, N.Y.

Inlander, C.B., et. al. (1988). Medicine On Trial: The Appalling Story of Medical Ineptitude and the Arrogance that Overlooks It. Prentice Hall Press, Simon & Schuster, NY.

Hiatt, H., Barnes, B., Brennan, T., et. al. (1989). A study of medical injury and medical malpractice. N Eng J Med, 321, 7, p. 480.

Annandale, E.. (1989). The malpractice crisis and the doctor-patient relationship. Sociology of Health and Illness, 11, 1, p.1.

Leape, L.L. (1989). Unnecessary surgery. Health Sciences Research, 24, 3, p. 351.

De La Serra, A. (1989). Iatrogenic illness: a prospective study. Mount Sinai Journal of Medicine, 56, 4, p. 267.

Brennan, T., et. al. (1990). Identification of adverse advents occurring during hospitalization. Ann of Int Med, 112, p. 221.

Brennan, T., et. al. (1991). Incidence of adverse events and negligence in hospitalized patients.Results of Harvard Medical Practice Study I, New Engl J Med, 324, 6, p. 377.

Leape, L.L., et. al. (1991). The nature of adverse events in hospitalized patients. Results of Harvard Medical Practice Study II, N Engl J of Medicine 325, 4, p. 245.

Monrad, Aas I. (1991). Malpractice. Quality Assurance in Health Care, 3, 1, p. 21.

Brennan, T. (1991). Practice guidelines and malpractice litigation: collision or cohesion.Health, Politics, Policy and Law, 16, 1, p. 67.

Localio, A., et. al. (1991). Relationship between malpractice claims and adverse events due to negligence. Results of Harvard Medical Practice Study III, N Eng J Med, 325, 4, p. 245.

Bogdanich, W. (1991) The Great White Lie: How America's Hospitals Betray Our Trust and Endanger Our Lives. Simon & Schuster, N.Y.

Franks, P., Clancy, C. (1992). Gatekeeping Revisited: Protecting patients from overtreatment. Health Affairs, 327, 6, p. 424.

Fruchter, J. (1993). Doctors on trial. Am J of Law and Medicine, 19, 4, p. 453.

Evans, R.S., et. al. (1993). Using a hospital information system to assess the effects of adverse drug events. Proc Ann Symp Comp Appl. Med Care, 17, p. 1.

Taragon, M. I., et. al. (1994). Does physician performance explain interspecialty differences in malpractice claims. Medical Care, 32, 7, p. 661.

Leape, L.L., Bates, D.W., et. al. (1995). System analysis of adverse drug events. JAMA, 274, 5, p. 35.

Kern, K.A. (1995). An overview of 711 general surgery liability cases: the anatomy of surgical malpractice. Bull of Am Coll of Surgeons, 80, 8, p. 34.

Smarr, L. (1996). Errors in diagnostic radiology. Presented at National Conference on Examining Errors in Health Care.

National Conference on Examining Errors in Health Care. (1996). Rancho Mirage Conference, October 15, 16, 1996.

Chilingerian, J. (1996). The nature of hospital care production process and medical errors. Presented at National Conference on Examining Errors in Health Care.

Classen, D., Pestatnick, S. (1997). Adverse drug events in hospitalized patients. JAMA, 277, 4, p. 301.

United States General Accounting Office. (1997). Medical Malpractice:Federal Tort Claims Act.. GAO/HEHS 97-57.

United States General Accounting Office. (1995). VA trends in malpractice claims. GAO/HRD 91-98.

United States General Accounting Office. (1995). Medical Liability: impact on hospital and physician costs. GAO/AIMD 95-169.

United States General Accounting Office. (1986). Medical Malpractice, no agreement on solutions. GAO/HRD 86-50.

United States General Accounting Office. (1993, 1986, 1992). Medical Malpractice. GAO/HRD 93-126, GAO/HRD 87-21, GAO/HRD 92-28l.

CHAPTER THREE: Lessons to be Learned

Bosh, C.L. (1979). Forgive and Remember: Managing Medical Failure. The University of Chicago Press, Chicago, Il.

Carew, T.C. (1981). Conditioning in a simple withdrawal reflex on the earthworm. Science, 175, p. 451.

Dautry -Varsat, A., et. al. (1984). How receptors bring proteins and particles into cells. Scientific American, May, 1984.

Mishkin, M., et. al. (1987) The Anatomy of Memory. Scientific American, Special Report.

Restak, R.M., (1988). The Mind. Bantam Books, NY.

Norman, D.A., (1988). The Design of Everyday Things. Basic Books, NY.

Gopher, D., et. al.. (1989). The nature and causes of human errors in a medical intensive care unit. Proceedings of the Human Factors Society, 33rd Annual Meeting, p. 356.

Roberts, K. (1990). Some characteristics of one type of high reliability organizations. Organization Science, 1, p. 160.

Reason, J.T. (1990). Human Errors. Cambridge University Press, N.Y.

Wingerson, L. (1990). Mapping Our Genes. Penguin Books, N.Y.

Kandel, E.R. (1991). Principles of Neural Science. Elsevier Sciences, N.Y.

Alexander, R.M. (1991). How Dinosaurs Ran. Scientific American, April 1991.

Chrousos, G.P., et. al. (1992). The concept of stress and stress system disorders. JAMA 267, 9, p. 1244.

Wilson, A.C., et. al. (1992). The recent African genesis of humans. Scientific American, April, 1992.

Welch, W.J. (1993). How cells respond to stress. Scientific American, May, 1993, p. 56.

Goldsmith, T.H. (1991). The Biological Roots of Human Nature. Oxford University Press, NY

Mooney, M.P. (1992). Human Anatomy Program, Summary Outlines in Anatomy and Physiology for First Year Students. University of Pittsburgh Press, Pittsburgh.

Somers, V.K., et. al. (1993). Sympathetic nerve activity during sleep. N Engl J Med, 328, 5, p. 303.

Paabo, S. (1993). Ancient DNA. Scientific American, November, 1993.

Changeux, J.P. (1993). Chemical signaling in the brain. Scientific American, November, 1993.

McGinnis, W., et. al. (1994). The molecular architects of body design. Scientific American, February, 1994.

Blumenthal, D. (1994). Making medical errors into medical treasures. JAMA, 272, 23, p. 1867.

Bogner, M.S. ed. (1994). Human Errors in Medicine. Laurence Erlbaum Associates, Hillsdale, NJ

Bogner, M.S.. (1994). Introduction in Human Errors in Medicine, ibid.

Leape, L.L. (1994). The preventability of medical injury. ibid.

Perper, J.A. (1994). Life threatening and fatal therapeutic misadventures. ibid.

Van Cott, H. (1994). Human errors: their causes and reduction. ibid.

Lo, B. (1994). Disclosing mistakes. in Problems in Ethics, Williams and Wilkins, Baltimore, p. 307.

Rosenthal, N. (1994). DNA and the genetic code. New Engl J Med, 331, 1, p. 39.

LeDoux, J. (1994). Emotion, memory and the brain. Scientific American, June, 1994, p. 50.

Raichle, M. E. (1994) Visualizing the mind. Scientific American, April, 1994.

Medina, J. (1994). Cloning the genes that govern circadian rythm. Psychiatric Times, July 1994.

Siegel, D. J. 1994. An overview of cognitive processes and memory Psychiatric Times, July, 1994.

Clayton, C., ed. (1995). The Human Body: An Illustrated Guide to It's Structure, Function and Disorders. Dorling Kindersley, N.Y.

Howard, S. (1996). Fatigue studies in medical personnel. Presented at National Conference on Examining Errors in Health Care, October 14, 1996.

Serig, D. (1996). Translating a human factor process from nuclear power plants to health care. Presented at National Conference on Examining Errors in Health Care, October 14, 1996.

Pierce, E., et. al. (1996). From human error to patient safety in anesthesia. Presented at National Conference on Examining Errors in Health Care, October 14, 1996.

Crawford, S., et. al. (1996). Examination of system factors associated with medication errors in hospitals. Presented at National Conference on Examining Errors in Health Care, October 14, 1986.

Phillips, D. (1999). New look reflects changing style of patient safety enhancement. JAMA, 281, 3, p. 217.

Helmreich, R. (1997). Managing human error in aviation. Scientific American Magazine, 1997.

CHAPTER FOUR: The Physician Industry

Billings, J.S. (1891). Ideals of medical education. Boston Medical Surgical Journal, 124, p. 619

Davis, J.S. (1892). To what extent should clinical instruction be afforded students of medicine in regular course. in JAMA, 19, p. 664, 1992. (from Journal of the American Medical Association One Hundred Years Ago). September 25, 1897. The advantages of a hospital internship. in JAMA, 278, 12, p. 962. (from JAMA One Hundred Years A Ago).

American Association of Medical Colleges, Annual Reports. (1961 to 1996). Section for Operational Studies. A.A.M.C., Chicago, Il,

King, H. (1970). Health in the medical and other learned professions. J. Chron Dis, 23, p. 257.

U.S. Department of Health, Education and Welfare, Health Resources Administration, Bureau of Health Manpower. (1978). A Report to the President and Congress on the Status of Health Professional Personnel in the U.S., HRA - 78-93, U.S. Govt Printing Office, Washington, D.C.

Schwartz, W.M., et. al. (1980). The changing geographic distribution of board certified physicians. Rand Notes, Rand Corporation, Santa Monica, CA.

Newhouse, J.P., et. al. (1982). How have location patterns of physicians affected the availability of medical services. Rand Notes, Santa Monica, CA.

U.S. General Accounting Office. (1984). Medicare, Physician Income by Specialty and Place of Service. GAO/HRD 86-90 BR, July 1986.

American Medical Association, Division of Survey and Data Resources. (1985). Physician Trends, AMA Chicago, IL.

Stillman, P.L., et. al. (1986). Assessing clinical skills of residents with standardized patients. Ann Intern Medicine, 105, p. 762.

Hillman, A.L. (1987). Financial incentives for physicians in HMO's: is there a conflict of interest. New Engl J Med, 317, p. 1743.

Stillman, P.L., et. al. (1987) A diagnostic fourth year medical student performance assessment. Arch Intern Med, 147, p. 1981.

AMA, Division of Survey and Data Resources. 1987. Physician Characteristics in the U.S. AMA, Chicago, IL.

Weiner, J.P. (1989). Forecasting physician supply and requirement in the U.S. Health Aff, 8, p.178.

Ginzberg, E. (1989) Physician supply in the year 2000. Health Aff, 8, 3, P. 84.

Levey, S., et. al. (1985). Bottom line health care? N Engl J Med, 312, p. 644.

Meyer, B.A. (1989). A student teaching module: physician errors. Fam Med, 21, p. 299.

Jonas, H.S., et. al. (1990). Undergraduate Medical Education. JAMA, 264, 7, p. 801.

Jolly, P., et. al. (1990). U.S. Medical School Finances. JAMA, 264, 7, p. 813.

Rowley, B.D., et. al. (1990). Graduate medical education in the U. S. JAMA, 264, 7, p. 822.

Association of American Medical Colleges. (1990). Report on Graduation Questionnaire of Class of 1990. AAMC, Chicago, IL.

American Medical Association. (1990, 1996). Socio-economic characteristics of Medical Practice. AMA, Chicago, IL.

Owens, A. (1990). Earnings make a huge breakthrough. Medical Economics, September 3, 1990.

Thorpe, K.E. (1990). House staff supervision and working hours.JAMA, 263, 23, p. 177.

Linton, A.J., et. al. (1990). Organized medicine and assessment of technology, (in Canada). N Engl J Med, 331, 17, p. 1167.

Iglehart, J.K. (1990). Congress moves to regulate self-referral and physicians' ownership of clinical laboratories. N Engl J Med, 322, 23, p. 168.

Hughes, P.H., et. al. (1991). Resident physicians substance abuse in the U.S. JAMA, 265, 16, p.2069.

Novack, D. H. (1997). Calibrating the physician: personal awareness and effective patient care. JAMA, 278, 6, p. 502.

Evidence Based Medicine Working Group. (1992). A new approach to teaching the practice of medicine. JAMA, 268, 17, p. 2420.

Enarson, C., et. al. (1992). An overview of reform initiatives in medical education 1906 through 1992. Medical Education Issue, 1992, JAMA, 268, 9, p. 1083.

People's Medical Society Newsletter. (1992). Doctors don't keep up. Newsletter 11, 6, p. 1, People's Medical Society, Allentown, PA.

Tannenbaum, S.J. (1993). What physician's know. N Engl J Med, 329, 17, p. 1268.

Eisenberg, J.M. (1993). Changing physician's practice. N Engl J Med, 329, 17, p. 1271.

Laine, C., et. al. (1993). The impact of regulation restricting medical house staff working hours on the quality of patient care. JAMA, 269, p. 374.

Wu, AW., et. al. (1993). Do house officers learn from their mistakes. JAMA, 265, p. 2089.

Dickler, R.M. (1998). Important challenges facing Academic Medicine and Academic Medical Centers. Speech presented by Senior Vice-President, Association of Medical Colleges, on December 10, 1998, at Medical College of Pennsylvania and Hahnemann School of Medicine, Phila., PA..

Iglehart, J.K. (1994). Physicians and the growth of managed care. N Engl J Med, 331, 17, p.1167.

Weiner, J.P. (1994). Forecasting the effects of health reform on U.S. physician workforce requirements. JAMA, 272, 3, p. 222.

Iglehart, J. K. (1994). Healthcare reform and graduate medical education. N Engl.J Med 330, 16, p. 116.

Petersdorf, R. G. (1994). Medical students and primary care. JAMA, 271, 12, p. 946.

U.S. Govt. Accounting Office. (1994). Millions loaned inappropriately to United States nationals at foreign medical schools. GAO/HEHS 94-28, January, 1994.

Seifer, S.D., et. al. (1995). Graduate medical education and physician practice location. JAMA, 274, p. 685.

Li, H. (1995). Physician Migration in Non-Metropolitan Counties of the United States from 1987 to 1990. University of North Carolina Press, Chapel Hill, N.C.

Mullan, F., et. al.. (1995). Medical migration and the physician work force. JAMA, 273, 19, p. 1521.

Kimball, H. R., et. al. (1995). Educational resource sharing and collaborative training in family practice and internal medicine. (A Statement from the American Boards of Internal Medicine and Family Practice). JAMA, 273, 4, p. 320.

Cohen, J.J. (1995). Academic medicine facing change. JAMA, 273, p. 244.

Woolhandler, S., et. al. (1995). Extreme risk - the corporate proposition for physicians. N Engl J Med, 333, 25, p. 1706.

Mangione, S., et. al. (1997). Cardiac auscultation skills of internal medicine and family practice trainees. JAMA, 278, 9, p. 696.

Tarlov, A.R. (1995). Estimating physician workforce requirements: The devil is in the assumptions. JAMA, 274, 19, p. 1558.

Iglehart, J. K. (1996). The quandary over graduates of foreign medical schools in the United States. New Engl J Med, 334, 25, p. 1679.

Lin, J.H. (1996). Academic medical center mergers. JAMA, 276, 21, p. 1768.

Riva, M. I., et. al. (1996). A report card on the physician work force in the United States. N Engl J Med, 334, 14, p. 892.

Baker, L. C. (1996). Differences in earnings between male and female physicians. N Engl J Med, 334, 15, p. 960.

Sonis, J., et. al. (1996). Teaching of human rights in United States medical schools. JAMA, 276, p. 1676.

Cantor, J.C., et. al. (1993). Preparedness for practice: young physicians' view of their professional education. JAMA, 270, 9, p.1035.

Barzansky, H.S., et. al., (1998). Educational programs in United States medical schools 1997. JAMA, 280, 9, p.788.

Dunn, M.R., et. al. (1998). Graduate medical education, 1997-1998. JAMA, 280, 9, p. 809.

Jones, R F., et. al. (1998). Review of United States medical school finances, (1997-1998). JAMA, 280, 9, p. 813.

Daugherty, S.R., et. al. (1998). Learning, satisfaction, mistreatment during medical internship. JAMA, 279, 15, p. 1194.

Martensen, R.L. (1997). The emergence of the hospital internship. (Journal of the American Medical Association 100 years ago). JAMA, 278, 12, p. 961.

Atwater, E.C. (1983). Making fewer mistakes: a history of students. Bull Hist Med, 57, p. 165.

CHAPTER FIVE: The Hospital Industry

Joint Commission Accreditation of Health Care Organizations. Accreditation Manual Series, JCAHO, Chicago, IL.

National Center for Health Statistics, Trends in Hospital Utilization in United States. Series 13. (1965-1990). U S Govt Printing Office, Washington, D.C.

Etzioni, A. (1974). Modern Organizations. Prentice Hall, N.J.

Starr, P. (1982). The Social Transformation of American Medicine. Basic Books, N.Y.

Wohl, S. (1984). The Medical Industrial Complex. Harmony Books, NY.

American Hospital Association. Annual Survey Data Base Hospitals. (1985, 1990, 1994, 1997). AHA, Chicago, IL.

Griffith, J.R. (1987). The Well Managed Community Hospital. Health Administration Press, Ann Arbor, MI.

Rosenberg, C. (1987). Care of Strangers: Rise of American Hospitals. J. Hopkins Press, Baltimore, Md.

Seay, J.D., et. al., ed.. (1988). In Sickness and In Health. McGraw-Hill Book Company, N.Y.

Rosner, D. (1988). Historical perspectives on the voluntary hospital, in In Sickness and In Health, Chapter 4, p. 87.

Curtin, L. (1989). Hospitals: back to the future or else? Nursing Management, 20, 12, p. 7.

Moran, E.J. (1990). Infection control investment saves in the long run. Hospitals, March 5, 1990, p. 58.

Bindman, A.B., et.al. (1990). A public hospital closes. JAMA, 264, 22, p. 2899.

Schulz, R., et. al. (1990). Management of Hospitals and Health Services. C.V. Mosby Company, NY.

Berwick, D.M., et. al. (1990). Hospital leaders' opinion of the HCFA mortality data. JAMA, 263, 2, p. 247.

Epstein, A.E. (1990). Do the poor cost more? A multi-hospital study of patient's socioeconomic status and use of hospital resources. N Engl J Med, 322, 16, p. 1122.

Park, R.E., et. al. (1990). Explaining variations in hospital death rates. JAMA, 266, 4, p. 484.

American Association of Medical Colleges. (1990-1996). United States Medical School Faculty. AAMC, Chicago, IL

Holm, S. (1989). Private hospitals in public systems. Hastings Center Report, September, 1989, p. 16.

Hadley, J., et. al. (1991). Comparison of uninsured and privately insured hospital patients. JAMA, 265, 2, p. 374.

Medical Economics. (1991). I'll take the ivory tower over a community hospital any day. Medical Economics, September 2, 1991.

Fye, W.B., (1991), The origin of the full time faculty system. JAMA, 265, 12, p. 1555.

Warren, E. (1991-1995). A Profile of Metropolitan Hospitals. American Hospital Association, Chicago, IL.

Mamon, J.D., et. al. (1992). Impact of hospital discharge planning on patient outcomes. Health Services Research, 27, 2, p. 156.

Iglehart, J.K. (1993). Teaching hospitals. N Engl J Med, 329, 14, p. 1052.

Inlander, C.B., et. al. (1993). Take This Book To The Hospital With You. A People's Medical Society Book, Allentown, PA.

Iglehart, J.K.. (1993). Rapid changes for academic medical centers, Part 1 and Part 2. N Engl J Med, 331, 20, p. 1391.

Consumer Check Book. (1994). Consumers' Guide to Hospitals. Center for the Study of Services, Washington, D.C.

Epstein, A.M. (1995). United States teaching hospitals in the evolving health care system. JAMA, 273, 15, p. 1203.

Kassirer, J.P. (1996). Tribulations and rewards of academic medicine: Where does teaching fit? N Engl J Med, 334, 3, p. 187.

Shea, S., et. al. (1996). Compensation to a Department of Medicine and its faculty members for the teaching of medical students and house officers. N Engl J Med, 334, 3, p. 162.

Meyer Sonis M.D.

Iezzoni, L.I. (1997). Major teaching hospitals defying Darwin. JAMA, 278, 6, p. 518.

CHAPTER SIX: The Doctor and Hospital Watchers

Dontell, H.N., et. al. (1984). Practitioner fraud and abuse in government medical benefit programs. Public Policy Research Organization, University of California, June 1984.

Dans, P.E., et. al. (1985). Peer review organizations: promises and pitfalls. N Engl J Med, 313, p. 1131.

Yessian, M. (1986). Medical Licensure and Discipline. Office of Inspector General: U.S. Department of Health and Human Services, Wash., DC.

Gray, B.H., ed. (1986). For Profit Enterprise in Health Care. National Academy Press, Washington, D.C., 1986.

Iglehart, J. (1987). Congress moves to bolster peer review: The Health Care Quality Improvement Act of 1986. N Engl J Med, 316, p. 961.

Relman, A. (1988). Assessment and accountability: the third revolution in medical care. N Engl J Med, 319, p. 1220.

Winslow, C.M., et. al.. (1999). Service quality in health care. JAMA, 260, 4, p.505.

Barnes, C., et. al. (1988). Accuracy of generic screens in identifying quality problems. Top Health Records Management 9, p. 72.

Vibbert, S. (1991). The Doctor Watchers. Grand Rounds Press, Whittle Direct Books, Knoxville, TN.

Cleary, P.D., et. al. (1992). A national survey of hospital patients: the relationship between reported problems with care and patient evaluations. Qual Rev Bull, 18, p. 53.

Galushi, B.L. (1989). Concentrating on the problem physician: perspectives in medical discipline. NY State J Med, 89, p. 209.

Siu, A.L., et. al. (1990). Patient, provider, and hospital characteristics associated with inappropriate hospitalization. Am J Publ Health, 80, 10, p. 1253.

American Association of Retired Persons. (1990). Recertification of health care professionals.

Citizen Advocacy News, AARP, 2, p. 1.

Lanning, J.A. (1990). The health care quality quagmire: some signposts. Hospital and Health Serv Adm, 35, 1, p. 39.

Wong, D.T., et. al., (1991). Predicting outcome in critical care: the current status of the APACHE scoring system. Canadian J of Anesthesia, 38, 3, p. 374.

Thomas, J.W., et. al. (1991). Measuring severity of illness: six severity systems and their ability to explain cost variations. Inquiry, 28, p. 39.

Pennsylvania Health Care Cost Containment Council. Hospital Effectiveness Reports: Annual (1991-1998). PA HCCC, Harrisburg, PA.

Federation of State Medical Boards of the United States. (1991). Official summary of reported board actions. JAMA, 267, 21, p. 2857.

Langsley, D.G. (1991). Recredentialling. JAMA, 265, 6, p. 772.

Gellham, A. (1991). Periodic physician recredentialing. JAMA, 265, 6, p. 752.

Mitchell, J.M. (1992). Physician ownership of physical therapy services. JAMA, 268, 15, p. 2055.

United States General Accounting Office. (1992). National Practitioner Data Bank. GAO/IMTEC 92-56, July, 1992.

Mullan, F., et. al. (1992). The National Practitioner Data Bank, Report from the first year. JAMA, 268, 1, p. 73.

Gray, J. (1992). Why bad doctors are not kicked out of medicine. Medical Economics, January 20, 1992, p. 126.

Mitchell, J.M., et. al. (1992). New evidence of the prevalence and scope of physician joint ventures. JAMA, 268, 1, p. 80.

Rubin, H.R., et. al. (1992). Watching the doctor watchers. JAMA, 267, 17, p. 2349.

Cleary, P.D. (1988). Patient satisfaction as an indicator of quality of care. Inquiry 25, p. 25.

United States General Accounting Office. (1993). National Practitioner Data Bank continues to experience problems. GAO/IMTEC 93-1, January, 1993.

Keystone Peer Review Organization. 1993. PRO Fourth Scope of Work Overview (1993-1996), Keystone Peer Review Organization, Harrisburg, PA.

Welch, H.G., et. al. (1994). Physician Profiling: practice patterns. N Engl J Med, 330, 9, p. 607.

Caulford, P.G., et. al. (1994). Physician incompetence: specific problems and predictors. Academic Medicine, 69, (supplement) 516, 1994.

Medical News and Perspectives. (1994). State Medical Boards discipline more, want role in Health system reform. JAMA, 271, 22, p. 1723.

DuBois, R.W. (1995). Hospital mortality as an indicator of quality in Goldfield, N. ed. Providing Quality Care: Future Challenges, 2nd ed., Health Administration Press, Ann Arbor, MI.

Wolfe, S., et. al. (1996). Questionable Doctors. Public Citizen's Health Research Group, Washington, D.C., March, 1996.

Kassirer, J.D. (1997). The new surrogate for Board certification. N Engl J Med, 337, 1, p. 43.

American Medical Association. (1997). American Medical Accreditation Programs. Accreditation Manual, AMA, Chicago, IL.

Medical News and Perspectives. (1997). National Committee for Quality Assurance (NCQA): Quality through evaluation. JAMA, 278, 19, p. 1555.

Medical News and Perspectives. (1997). Health Care Financing Administration (HCFA) focuses on new plans for quality care. JAMA, 278, 19, p. 1559.

Medical News and Perspectives. (1997). Institute for Healthcare Improvement (IHI) views collaboration vs. competition in quality. JAMA, 278, 19, p. 1560.

Medical News and Perspectives. (1997). National Patient Safety Foundation studies systems. JAMA, 278, 19, p. 1561.

Medical News and Perspectives. (1997). Joint Commission (JCAHO) begins tracking outcome data. JAMA, 278, 19, p. 1562.

Iezzoni, L.I. (1997). The risks of risk adjustment. JAMA, 278, 19, p. 1600.

Brook, R.H. (1997). Managed care is not the problem, Quality is. JAMA, 278, 19, p. 1612.

Dehlindorf, C.E., et. al. (1998). Physicians disciplined for sex-related offenses. JAMA, 279, 23, p. 1883.

Chassin, M.R., et. al. (1998). The urgent need to improve health care quality. Institute of Medicine National Round Table on Health Care Quality. JAMA, 280, 11, p. 1000.

Psychiatric News. (1999). American Medical Accreditation Program: A national benchmark for assessing physician quality. Psychiatric News, 34, 5, March 5, 1989.

Meyer Sonis M.D.

APPENDIX B

INFORMED PATIENT RESOURCES

<u>Personal Medical File</u>

All too often patients have relied heavily on their physicians and hospitals to be the sole repository for the records, reports, studies which have been generated during the course of their medical care. However, the nature of medical practice and hospital care today suggests the need for a patient to become more informed about his/her own and his/her family's medical history and medical care received. Thus it behooves an informed patient to develop and maintain his/her family's personal medical file repository. Such a repository can range from the very simple system to a very detailed and elaborate system. There are several excellent sources which can be of help in guiding an informed patient to develop such a personal medical file repository.

(1.) How To Keep Your Own Medical Record, page 329-336, in Getting The Most For Your Medical Dollar, published 1991, a People's Medical Society Book, 462 Walnut Street, Allentown, PA 18102.
(2.) Medical Records, Getting Yours, A Consumer Guide to Obtaining and Understanding Medical Records, 1995, A Public Citizen's Health Research Group Publication, 1600 20th Street, N.W., Washington, D.C., 20009.
(3.) Keeping Track, A Personal Health Record System, by Eleanor Laumark, Victoria Christianson, 1980, published by Woodbridge Press Publishing Company, P.O.B. #6189, Santa Barbara, CA, 93111.

Personal Medical Library

All too often patients have relied exclusively on their physicians and hospital personnel to provide them with information about their health, medical conditions, medical care and to aid them in understanding this information. The nature of medical and hospital practice today suggests the importance to the informed patient of becoming more familiar himself or herself with some basic rudimentary information about their health, medical conditions, medical care. Thus it behooves such a patient to develop a personal medical library or seek access to such a medical library through public libraries and/or patient education programs offered by a local hospital. There are several sources which can serve the informed patient as a basic compendium of medical information.

(1.) Clinical Anatomy and Pathophysiology for the Health Professional by Joseph Stewart, M.D., 1990, Medmaster, Inc., P.O.B. 640028, Miami, FL, 33164.
(2.) Merck Manual of Diagnosis and Therapy, 1992, published by Merck Research Laboratories, West Point, PA, 19486.
(3.) Patient's Guide for Medical Tests, Barry Zaret, M.D., ed., 1997, Yale University of Medicine, published by Houghton Mifflin, 222 Berkeley Street, Boston, MA, 02116.
(4.) A Consumer Reference, Everything You Need to Know About Medical Tests, 1996, published by Springhouse Corp., 1111 Bethlehem Pike, P.O.B. 908, Springhouse, PA, 19477-0908.
(5.) The PDR Family Guide to Prescription Drugs, 1994, published by Medical Economics, 5 Paragon Drive, Montvale, NJ, 07645.
(6.) The Consumer's Medical Desk Reference, 1995, by Charles Inlander, The People's Medical Society,

published by Hyperion, 114 Fifth Avenue, New York, NY, 10011.
(7.) Teaching Patients with Acute Symptoms and Teaching Patients with Chronic Symptoms, 1992, published by Springhouse Corporation, 1111 Bethlehem Pike, P.O.B. 908, Springhouse, PA, 194776-0908.
(8.) Good Operations Bad Operations, 1993, a book of The People's Medical Society, published by Viking, 375 Hudson Street, New York, NY, 10014.

Organizational Resources For Informed Patients.

During the past decade, and for a variety of reasons not the least of which was the complexity and impersonal nature of medical care and the expectations of patients from their medical care providers, increased attention has been focused on the need for more active participation of patients in their own medical care. Pursuant to this trend there has been an explosion in the number and type of organizational resources available to help a patient become a partner in his/her own medical care. These resources were such as to: provide a patient with information about safe health behavior, their health, the medical care they receive; enable a patient to participate with other patients, manifesting similar medical problems in self-help groups; allow patients to receive emotional support from each other in managing their chronic disabling medical conditions; foster development of patient advocacy organizations. Such resources, for example, ranged from tele-med audio tapes on various medical problems which a patient can secure by a phone call, to publications of governmental agencies at a national, state, local level, to membership organizations for patient consumers in the form of advocacy groups. Because of the vast number of such resources now available to the consumers of medical care it is almost impossible to find one source which can provide an exhaustive list of such resources. For this reason I will cite but a

Skeletons in the Medical Closet
A Personal Story and a Professional Report

few of such resources below; a more comprehensive listing will be available to the reader of this book on request, as per my letter to a reader.

(1.) People's Medical Society
   462 Walnut Street
   Allentown, PA, 18102

A non-profit consumer health organization, founded in 1985. This organization has developed an excellent reputation for its advocacy of patient rights and patient information. The PMS has produced and disseminated health information of pertinence to consumers of health services. In addition to its periodic bulletins, several of its books are outstanding resources of information. Attention is called to Getting The Most of Your Medical Dollar, Take This Book to the Hospital With You, Your Medical Rights, Medicine on Trial, The Consumer's Medical Desk, Good Surgery-Bad Surgery.

(2.) National Patient Safety Foundation of the
   American Medical Association
   515 North State Street
   Chicago, IL, 60610

A non-profit organization, founded in 1997, for the purpose of collecting information regarding the safety of medical care and for dissemination of this information to the public.

(3.) Public Citizen
   600 20th Street, N.W.
   Washington, D.C., 20009

A non-profit organization founded in 1971. The Public Citizen's Health Research Group, of the Public Citizen Organization, has focused its efforts on behalf of consumer

Meyer Sonis M.D.

rights for safe and secure health care. Their publications and newsletters are an excellent health information source.

(4.) Food & Drug Administration
   Office of Consumer Affairs
   5600 Fisher's Lane, HFE 88
   Rockville, MD, 20857

A federal governmental agency which can provide information for the consumer of medical care about the safety of drugs, medical devices.

(5.) Office of Disease Prevention and Health Promotion
   National Health Information Center
   P.O.B. 1133
   Washington, D.C., 20013-1133

A federal governmental agency which can provide the consumer of medical care with information of pertinence.

(6.) National Self-Help Clearinghouse
   Graduate School and University Center
   City University of New York
   25 W. 43rd Street., Room 620
   New York, NY 10036

A non-profit agency which can provide the consumer of medical care with information regarding self-help groups.

(7.) United States Government Printing Office, Washington, D.C., 20402-9325

Interested persons can receive a periodic update on publications available regarding topics pertinent to medical care.

Finding Medical Help on The Internet

With the ever increasing pace of development of the information highway, a new source for information and help has become available to consumers of medical care. Each day new possibilities emerge with the latest one in June, 1999, *drkoop.com*. As with printed information for the consumer of medical care, the lists of possibilities is quite extensive so that I will cite but a few examples while referring the reader to my Letter to the Reader.

(1.) American Medical Association, http:/www.ama-assn.org
 A site with links to consumer health information.
(2.) Medicine Net, http:/www.medicinenet.com
 A very content rich commercial site which includes interactive groups.
(3.) OncoLine, http:/www.oncolink.upenn.edu
 A huge collection of cancer information and links based at the University of Pennsylvania.
(4.) drkoop.com
 A most comprehensive consumer help resource about health, medical organizations.

Meyer Sonis M.D.

Letter To My Readers

My Dear Reader,

In my decision to prepare this manuscript it had been my intent to disseminate information to the reading public about the safety of their medical hospital care. On my completion of this manuscript it is now my hope to serve as a <u>P</u>hysician <u>A</u>dvocate <u>F</u>or <u>I</u>nformed <u>P</u>atients through the ultimate development and operation of a symbolic store and it's PAFIP program. In other words an additional path for dissemination of information from the medical information highway.

Through such a PAFIP store I would hope to serve as a medical information guide to two audiences, namely: the human service practitioners (whether physicians, nurses, social workers, psychologists, others) who may be interested in serving as physician or human service practitioner advocate for informed patients; the patients or clients who need to become more informed about their health, health behavior, medical problems, doctors and hospitals.

Through such a PAFIP store, activities will take place which would be aimed at exciting the interest of all human service practitioners in voluntarily pledging to serve as an advocate for informed patients in their own practices.

Through such a PAFIP store, educational material would be available to human service practitioners which would be focused on the medical education of patients or clients in order to aid them to become more informed. A sample of such PAFIP snippets of information, currently in preparation, include: a series of Physician Practice Guidelines For Medical Education of Patients During Office Visits, Hospitalization, Clinical Consultation; a series of Physician Practice Guidelines For the Medical Education of Parents About the Medical and Hospital Care of Their Children; a series of Human Service Practitioner

Skeletons in the Medical Closet
A Personal Story and a Professional Report

Practice Guidelines For Education of Patients/Clients in Non Medical Settings; Human Science Practitioner Practice Guidelines For Collaboration With Medical Settings.

Through the PAFIP store I would be available to directly respond to requests for information from the consumer of medical and hospital servers about their becoming more informed patients. Educational material would be available to these persons on: setting up a personal medical file and medical library; home record keeping of medical information; securing lists of resources (such as self-help groups, patient advocacy agencies, governmental information regarding health/medical problems); securing copies of a medical or hospital record filing medical complaints, various diseases or disorders or medical problems, choosing a doctor or hospital, understanding your own medical record or hospital record. In serving as a medical information guide to patients of medical and hospital care, the PAFIP store would not be serving as a personal physician but rather as an informational guide to aid them in making more effective use of their doctors and hospitals.

In keeping with my wish to serve as a physician advocate for more informed patients I would welcome any comments from the readers of this book and letters about the usefulness of this book to them, questions which the book may have raised, their own experiences with medical and hospital care, and further information which they may be seeking. I will respond to all comments and/or requests received as quickly as possible.

                     Sincerely yours,

                     Meyer Sonis, M.D.
                     Physician Advocate for
                     Informed Patients
                     40B Long Beach Boulevard
                     Loveladies, N.J. 08008

Meyer Sonis M.D.

ABOUT THE AUTHOR

- Fifty-five years of experience as a physician since medical school education.

- Personal experiences with medical misadventures.

- Professional experience as a clinician (general practitioner and pediatric psychiatrist specialist), medical educator, administrator of a medical facility, and medical officer of an academic medical center responsible for monitoring quality assurance programs of hospitals.

- Served on federal and state medical task forces, commissions, committees, conferences.